YOU ARE AS SICK AS YOUR SECRETS

Trauma Understands Trauma

Deirdre Rolfe

A catalogue record for this book is available from the National Library of Australia

ISBN Paperback:978-0-6457325-0-4
Hardcopy ISBN:978-0-6457325-1-1
Ebook ISBN:978-0-6457325-2-8

Interior images, photography: Deirdre Rolfe
Designer: Lee Walker
Editor: Jess Lomas

Dedicated to my mother, 'Heather' Harriot MacIntosh, a scraggly bush that can survive anywhere. Your love, psychological training, intuitive, creative talents, humour and sheer grit for survival is the reason I am.

Contents

I suppose a ten-year-old girl shouldn't feel so indifferent when her father, holding a gun pointed at the middle of her forehead, pulls the trigger. But abuse is funny that way. My adult self reflects in total awe and with surreal disbelief that somehow the gun jammed that night. I got to live!

Chapter 1
I Got to Live

We were on our boat in The Bahamas, anchored off from Eleuthera. Mother and Father had been drinking that night. I recall there was hardly a night when they weren't. My father warned me before we all went downstairs to bed that I was not allowed to get up in the middle of the night. He mumbled something about pirates in the area. I was ten. When I got up for a glass of water, I was standing at the top of the stairwell and saw my father peering up at me with a gun cocked and pointed towards my forehead.

I froze.

He pulled the trigger.

It jammed.

I remember thinking, surely he saw me? Why would he pull the trigger? Was that an accident? Did he do it on purpose? It didn't make sense.

Immediately he started yelling, 'Look what you made me do! I almost killed you! Do you see what you've done?'

I felt sorry for him. I was worried he would find it difficult to cope with what he just did. We never spoke of it, ever. I doubt my mother ever knew. I doubt he even gave it a second thought. The most disturbing part of that story to me is not that my father almost killed me, it's that a little ten-year-old girl was more concerned that her father would be burdened by his actions. It's the starkness in the girl who didn't even flinch because trauma by that age was a normal event.

This is my story. It's my parents' story. It is my intention as I tell the story that it links to many stories, my own and yours, the reader. The story you see is fixed in its truth. However, through the narrative, the words and the tone, it can be woven into something hauntingly beautiful. A tapestry hanging proudly, its intricate patterns created by those who conquered the fiercest battles. I would hang that tapestry backwards, as the truth is not in the perfect image.

Trauma hides, it is found in the chaos behind an interwoven mess of knotted, hanging threads. The true journey is in the complexities of fear, pain, anger, grief, shame, illusions, reconciliation and lack of reconciliation, forgiving versus unforgiving, choice, hard work, hope, expression, truth, vulnerability, acceptance, courage, standard, grace, humility and love. This is where the real story lives. That is the story I am here to tell.

It is not important or even possible that I list every grave or morose memory. This is not written to trigger you or to make my trauma the focus of this book. You are the focus. Through my own story, I hope to pave the way to how one can navigate through the darkness of trauma and the web of secrets.

I invite you on a journey into my mind as a survivor of abuse. As a counsellor specialised in trauma for over twenty-five years, I will offer my perspective as the victim, survivor and as a therapist to thousands who have bravely shared their own stories of trauma. I will highlight many of the tools I developed along the way, whether they were gathered by my own innate survival, gifted by strangers, friends or passed down by my mother, herself a talented therapist. Tools I've developed from years of studies in East, West, Celtic, Norse, Caribbean and Mexican belief systems or passed down through my cultural lineage of Scottish/English/German/Norse descendants. I was looking for anything mind, body or spirit that could lead to the path of healing myself and ultimately others. After all, my life was not a straight path but a fight along sharp uncertain corners, steep unrelenting inclines, turbulent declines and many cliff edges. Why would I expect my studies, my quest for answers and the tools of navigation that would save my life and keep me from falling off the edge to be anything linear?

I invite you to be a witness to the way I perceive things and how I learned to reframe, integrate, rebuke, cast out, re-author, reprogram, reclaim, release, stand up, armour up and how I finally created a life in which I no longer had to fight for my right to be. I invite you to stand in the ring of fire with me, beside me, as we proudly voice our truth and share the stories that threaten to define us. These are the narratives we can take hold of and rewrite into the wellness of our bodies, our minds, our identity, our souls and our destiny as we reclaim the life and person that so dangerously almost got snuffed out.

It is my hope that sharing my story will inspire you to pause when meeting others and remind you to be kinder, always, as love is our only hope. Remember that some of the deepest wounds belong to those who are the loudest, brightest, funniest or deemed too much.

Challenging your own foibles, insecurities, hurts and unresolved subconscious triggers, I invite you onto the pathway toward a better, more conscious humaning. Much more than just being a human, humaning is the *ing*, the action of doing: loving, giving, supporting, sharing, truthing, rewarding, creating and celebrating being human.

A Secret (noun): Something that is kept or meant to be kept unknown or unseen by others.[1]

There were so many secrets in my family. Inherited long before I was even born, we were raised to hold them close. I do not believe it is personally cathartic or beneficial to others that all of one's secrets are revealed. This forced purging under the guise of therapy or spiritual enlightenment is dangerous. Deep traumas and secrets buried in the subconscious mind are often done so in self-preservation. This is the wonderful power of your subconscious mind, whose job is to protect you—let it! Opening vaults or revealing all would not only flood your body and mind with a tsunami of emotions strong enough to crack you, but it would also leave you open to re-injury.

---

[1] Oxford English Dictionary.n.d.www.oed.com (Accessed February 24, 2023).

The real problem with keeping some secrets, however, is you continue to carry them. Not facing them and doing the work within yourself passes the responsibility of those burdens onto others. One cannot hide such hauntings as they seep out through your behaviours, choices, relationships, projections, attachments and re-enactments, bleeding into the next generation, until someone digs deep, draws them out and holds them up to the light. Exploring them, understanding and accepting them can then begin the process of watering them down.

There is no cure for such sufferings but the watering down through the generations allows them to fade away, so much so it can feel like a cure. This can only happen, however, by consciously acknowledging they exist, as they belong to a part of you that has been dying to tell their stories. It involves waking up from the slumber of denial and the darkness they have hidden in for so long; buried in shame and fear, they only sink deeper.

This is my goal, the real intention in my endless pursuits for truth, self-awareness, self-actualisation and my purpose for my family, clients and all those who seek more. I do it in the hope that one day, as my picture holds the helm of the family tree, those generations after me will be better, live freer, feel and be healthier. They will be proud of their history, of the legacy of their name and of the standard I did my best to reclaim, for me and for them. I will pass the baton, knowing I did all I could to clear the inherited debt that left my family so deficit; two out of us four siblings died far too early. Under the insurmountable weight of the secrets they ingested, their minds were haunted and their bodies ravaged until they just couldn't take anymore. Some secrets, therefore, must be brought to the surface and forced to face the light of truth, set free in the narrative of the only person who has the right to tell it—the victim; a word used to describe many of us who have endured trauma.

Victim (*noun*) (1): one that is injured, destroyed or sacrificed under any of various conditions (2): one that is subjected to oppression, hardship or mistreatment (3): one that is tricked or duped.
Synonyms: casualty, fatality, loss, prey[2]

I have never been fond of the word victim. It is a powerful word, used to describe the subjective and collective experience that gives voice to what we endured, however long-term we risked identifying with it.

We are not our trauma, but we have experienced trauma. If left too long the word victim festers into a permanent fabric of who we have been told we are, rather than who we choose to be. Imagine the residual destruction to one's psyche if imprinted with the belief that they are a casualty, fatality, loss or prey. When we go to the undercurrents of words, we find deeper meaning unseen to the conscious mind but inherently understood by the subconscious. Therefore, a casualty is an injured soul; a fatality is death to whom you could have been,

---

[2] Merriam-Webster. 2022. "Merriam-Webster Dictionary." www.merriamr-webster.com (Accessed February 24, 2023).

loss is to a part that will always leave you seeking and prey is the perpetual victim. How we go about transcending the word victim and many other disempowering, devaluing, demoting and destructive words will be discussed later. For now, I will use the word victim from the experiencing point of reference only.

I strongly believe trauma victims need to be heard, seen, witnessed and provided with tools for expression both verbally, subconsciously and somatically. Not having therapy can lead to mental health, relationship and identity issues, as well as severe health complications later in life. The mind and body can only take so much. The fear of reaching out is still a reality for many, however. Not telling and maintaining secrets is a learned or trained behaviour and becomes a survival instinct. It's sustained by fear of further abuse or retributions. Unspoken contracts were made in exchange for favouritism, money or mere survival because of the belief no one would come to your rescue. Signed in blood, that belief formed because no one ever did. Even when those brave souls reach out later in life, many fail to continue the arduous journey of expression, truth or therapy. Their worst fears are realised when they finally tell their story to the person who doesn't have the tools to receive it.

There is a panel of judges sitting in the minds of the untrained individuals who show up in various forms as: therapists, doctors, friends, families and lovers. Intentional or not, they view the symptoms of trauma as neurosis, embellishments, a blithe on your character or even an undiagnosed mental health issue. The victim can see it in their eyes, hear it in the tone of their voice and feel it in the energy that congests the space. That judgement is very painful to a victim of trauma. They have already endured years of not being heard, seen or believed. In fact, their mere survival was dependent on developing this acute and uncanny sixth sense. At times a gift, at times a burden, one can't simply turn it off. It can make casual social events or relationships challenging. Sensing how one really thinks and feels isn't always pleasant. It is the ability to see every micro-expression, hear the slightest distinctions in one's tone of voice, what is said behind the words, feel the shifts in mood and read behind the eyes. Who a person is and who a person isn't is always in the eyes.

The symptoms of trauma, raw and unhealed, are deemed by many as ugly, unfitting or just too much. A tsunami of rapid speech and body tics vomit out wildly in a fury of untamed, incongruent and fragmented pieces. It looks like, sounds like and is chaos. It is dark, complex and has many layers that create cognitive dissonance in the victim. This imbues a sense of unreality, confusion and a mindset of not trusting their perception of the abuse, the relationship to the perpetrator and ultimately all relationships, past and present. It can leave the victim vulnerable and exposed to more abuse from other covert predators that sniff out and prey on their exposed vulnerabilities. Cyclical patterns may have formed, creating attachment issues where the victim unconsciously reverts to the child and the lover becomes their parent. Desperately fearing abandonment, rejection and judgment, they work harder for those who dismiss, denounce or devalue them. This is a dangerous web many victims often find themselves lured into as predators so easily recognise their malleable boundaries.

Imagine receiving a puzzle with pieces missing and there are no instructions, not even a lid with a picture to reference. This is the starting point for both the victim and the therapist working with them. Therefore, it takes skill. It takes time. It takes a mind, body, spiritual approach, incorporating a multitude of evidence-based therapies and mindful, creative and 'embodied' modalities.

There is no one measurement of trauma as it is defined as an umbrella of conscious, subconscious and body-felt sensing, experienced at a psychological, physical, emotional, sensory, intuitive and energetic level. How one defines trauma is a subjective choice and right. The incongruence of how trauma is experienced gets encoded through our senses like shards of broken glass. These fragmentations regurgitate through: nightmares, triggers, somatic tics, re-enactments, learned helplessness, abusive relationships, avoidant attachment styles, alcohol /drug abuse, over-eating, hyper-sexual activity, nervous system hyper and hypo arousal, fight, flight and freeze responses, shame, feeling unlovable, abandonable, not good enough, not worthy, cognitive distortions, procrastination, foggy brain, not feeling safe, dissociation, de-personalisation, de-realisation, anger, revenge, resentment, embitterment, depression, anxiety, co-dependency, constant scanning (distrust), sleep issues and a sense of being different from everyone else.

Trauma is the belief there is no bottom, no limit to the sadistic perpetrator's ability of power; that regardless of how bad things get it can always get worse—and did. There is always another level.

Trauma is also defined as:

'Psychological Trauma is the unique individual's experience of an event of enduring conditions in which the individual's ability to integrate his or her emotional experience is overwhelmed (i.e., His or Her ability to stay present, understand what is happening, integrate the feelings and make sense of the experience) or the individual's experiences (subjectively). A threat to life, bodily integrity, or sanity.'[3]

'An inescapably stressful event that overwhelms people's existing coping mechanisms.'[4]

'Traumatic events can lead to physical and mental health conditions including heart attacks, strokes, obesity, diabetes, cancer, autoimmune disease, PTSD and chronic inflammation.'[5]

Since I was three years old, I always coloured just outside the lines. Through the stories I've been told or from my own

---

[3] Giller, E. (1999) *What Is Psychological Trauma?* Sidran Institute. Available at: https://www.sidran.org/wp-content/uploads/2019/04/What-Is-Psychological-Trauma.pdf (Accessed: February 24, 2023).

[4] van der Kolk, B. A., and R. Fisler. 1995. 'Dissociation and the Fragmentary Nature of Traumatic Memories: Overview and Exploratory Study' *Journal of Traumatic Stress.* United States National Library of Medicine 8, no. 4: 505–25. https://doi.org/10.1007/BF02102887.

[5] Harvard Health Publishing.February 12, 2021.'Past Trauma May Haunt Your Future Health.'Harvard Health. https://www.health.harvard.edu/diseases-and-conditions/past-trauma-may-haunt-your-future-health (Accessed: February 24, 2023).

memories, I identified a few small but poignant things I innately carried which I now know are the beginning staples of resiliency:

- Intuition
- Courage to step outside the lines
- Innate optimism
- Innate empathy
- A sense of humour
- Deep gratitude
- A sense I was a micro part of something macro
- An insatiable need to TALK
- A keen observer
- The courage to stand back up

I've had moments of serendipity throughout my life where one person somehow appeared at the right time and gave me a gift in a word, a sentence or a phrase that altered the direction I took. Those are the sliding door moments. I have always recognised them as destiny sending me a message, perhaps from my deceased ancestors, reminding me that I am OK; that despite what I was experiencing, somehow hope was mine to behold and that I didn't deserve it and I would get through it. It's been my life's work to understand why not everyone survives their trauma. I've seen firsthand what a soul looks like when it breaks. The measurement is seen in the eyes and sensed, felt and heard in the micro expressions of the body; a sound so loud it's inaudible.

I've seen trauma kill through years of depression, self-harm, binge eating, anorexia, addictions, immunity issues, self-sabotage, mental health, shame, grief, low worth, lack of reconciliation, secrets, or the final stages of disease—heart attacks and cancer; the nervous system can only handle so much.

I don't subscribe to quick fixes or 'cures' of such layered and systematic complexities, however, with the right tools you can be well. It's the kind of well where joy fills the marrow of your bones, where love can feel safe, where home exists and where you can truly connect to the incredible, worthy, beautiful human being you are.

I am not your guru, nor do I profess my system is the only way or the cure to all that ails you. I am one of you, a child of extreme trauma, a woman who has had far more regurgitations of that past than she ever deserved. I do not believe in the saying 'life doesn't give you more than you can handle'. I know it can smash you and knock you down until you are face-planted on the ground. But there is a way to stand back up. Whether you do it in leaps and bounds or in tiny micro steps, the forward motion is the energy toward you rescuing yourself. Always, just keep moving forward.

In this book, I will take off the cloak of my identity as a therapist of twenty-five years and stand up to face my own vulnerabilities, fears, lessons, battles and secrets in my family. It is the foundation of my work, my passion, my mission, my purpose and at the deepest core of who I am.

Every morning I wake up, I stand up. I stand up for my mother, my precious gem, who endured a childhood of trauma only to sustain another fifty-eight years of a marriage riddled with abuse. I stand up for my sister, who died too soon under the insurmountable trauma she couldn't find her way out of. I stand up for my brother, who died only months after my sister;

a victim of extreme and complex trauma that shook the essence of his mind for most of his adult life. I stand up for every client that bravely comes to see me and entrusts me with their journey. I stand up for everyone who still feels shame, fear, disconnected, unsafe and unheard or is lost in their own self-destructive inherent patterns.

I stand up for me.

I am me.

I am you.

So, take my hand and walk with me, beside me. Let me share my truth, the truth I hope will begin the process of you standing up for yourself.

Chapter Two
Trauma is Viewed with a Wide Lens to Get the Full Angle

We all know the key to a good home is the foundation it's built on. There is a clear and consistent image in my head of what I always thought that foundation was. It's a picture of when my mother and father first met. My father is seated on a couch and my mother is curled up next to him, both look very Hollywood with their stunning looks and debonair style of clothes. This photo was highlighted in every lounge room of every house we grew up in. It was the photo all guests would see; all anniversaries would be referenced to and their final obituaries were held to. A standard of love, beauty, sexiness, grace and class one couldn't help but envy. This photo represented their entire fifty-eight years, the glue that helped bind them together despite all the dark escapades, traumas, secrets and dysfunctions. This photo held the story they both wanted told and was the default image I conjured up in my mind whenever I questioned the why of their coupling. Why did she stay? Why did no one ever investigate our wellbeing beyond that image, despite the overwhelming evidence to do so?

Pictures don't lie, but the human mind is such we are conditioned to see what we want to see. This photo is their first secret, one of many and the beginning of the sickness in our family. We are all as sick as our secrets.

My parents: 'Heather' Harriot Rolfe and Phillip William Rolfe.

A day after my mother died, my father chose this picture for her obituary. I looked at it lovingly, as I had for many decades. At least in the beginning, she was loved, I thought. It was taken just before they got married. He told me this wasn't their place after all. It belonged to a friend of his, a colleague from his early work in an insurance company. He and my mother were over for drinks. The dog, he cheerfully explained, isn't even theirs. My father told me he was staring at the girlfriend of his work colleague. He proclaimed, with a wry grin, 'You know

Deirdre, I never met a woman I didn't want to fuck and I really wanted to fuck her'. A picture tells a thousand words but only to the subjective experience of the viewer.

SECRET #1

This photo is not the beginning of their big love story. We were sitting at the long oak table at one of my Father's homes in Ajijic, Mexico. It was the same table from my childhood, as he had it shipped to all his primary residences around the world over many years. He was in his usual spot at the head of the table, drinking copious amounts of tea served to him by the house man, Armando. I remember thinking, 'I'm forty years old, my mother just died, he will be fine.' He had insisted I leave the hotel I'd been staying at for the last several months, sitting bedside vigil to my dying mother. Crumbling cookies onto his plate and the floor, he was going over the rules for breakfast. It was the morning after she passed and he wanted me to understand how to cook him his perfect egg. It wasn't a new conversation, but the oddity and obsessiveness of the finer details were even more controlling than I remembered.

'Take the egg pan under the cupboard designed to fit the perfect fried egg. The edge must be crispy, but the yolk must be runny. Are you listening Deirdre? You haven't a clue, do you? Now, I do not want to smell the egg cooking, do you understand?'

'Um, I'm not going to even attempt that,' I mumbled. 'I'm sure you've trained Armando to do it.'

'Yes, Armando does a perfect egg, but it took him thirty bloody years and I still smell it.'

At that moment the doorbell rang, a loud base tone echoed in the hallway due to the cathedral ceilings and shiny white tiles. Armando, now aged beyond his fifty years, likely from my father's abuse and his not-very-secretive penchant for alcohol, walked sideways with a slightly hunched back as he answered the door. A man dressed in a black suit handed him an urn— my mother's ashes were delivered. I couldn't believe how fast it all happened, Father said something about disease control. He placed the ashes right in front of me and continued to talk about the perfect egg without flinching. His bizarre unreality, his abuse or complete lack of any empathetic connection completely unfettered by my mother now reduced to ash gnawed at my soul.

'Now, if you want breakfast it is served at eight a.m., if you are here at five minutes before eight you will not be served. If you are here five minutes after eight you will not be served, do you understand?'

I started crying, deep, body surges causing me to gasp for air. I just couldn't stay where each word he spoke sucked the air out of the room.

'THAT'S MY MUM!' I shouted. Visibly shaken and tears welling, my jaw felt tight and my back had flames raging up my spine. I abruptly stood up, pushed my chair into place as I had been trained to do since age three and ran off to my room. I screamed my cries into my pillow, drenching it with tears for my mother, the tears of the little girl in me who was strained by the never-ending abuse. I cried at the images that were surging through my mind of my frail eighty-year-old mother that starkly reminded me of the covert abuse she faced in the details of his reactions, inactions, deliberate distractions and just how much more she endured between the cracks. My niece, his grand-daughter, Valentia, who was also staying at the house, sat at the table having witnessed the conversation.

'What's wrong with her?' my father asked.

'Grandpa, her mum just died, hours ago, the ashes were placed right in front of her, she's grieving.'

'Still?' he queried.

Later that afternoon, Father asked for assistance in writing the obituary for his now-deceased wife. He enlisted me, his grandchildren and my older sister Heidi to send him emails with personally written paragraphs reflecting her life, the emotions around her death and the final days at the hospital—something he didn't know much about as he only visited her once in hospital; he simply said he just didn't like them. The one time he did go, he bought an enormous vase with fifty-eight roses to represent their fifty-eight years together. Mother's eyes lit up and Father was especially chuffed at the responses he got from the doctors and nurses commending him for such a thoughtful act.

While Father was at home, I spent every day with my mother during those months at her hospital bedside. I'd often check in, worried he wasn't coping with what anyone would imagine was incomprehensible grief. However, he behaved like a cheeky boy. Later that afternoon, sitting at that long oak table, he showed me many photos of the women who responded to his local ad for an older gentleman looking for a travel companion. It seemed he had a photo shoot, as he showed me photos of him on his iPad wearing a tailored blue jacket, hair greased back, his white dentures brilliantly reflecting the light from the afternoon sun, his mansion with its large roman columns and a crystal-clear pool in the background. He looked wealthy and dressed to impress. 'Armando took those photos,' he smirked.

Apparently, Father found the time to interview these women at his home. The woman he chose looked to be around mid-fifties, blonde with large, enhanced breasts, a dark tan, a red plunging V-neck dress and a penchant for chunky gold jewellery.

'She lives in Las Vegas,' he chimed in. 'I wasn't sure you'd understand, my needs?' he smiled.

My bubble burst. He got me yet again. I was still filling in the narrative, telling a different story based on what I just thought 'normal' was, or perhaps it was still what I hoped it could be. My father was consistent but even now, after all these years, my mind couldn't follow the abrupt black-and-white thinking that felt like it was always kept on ice. How apt, I thought, as it was exactly how he liked his scotch—straight, chilled and served in a very expensive crystal glass. Money always set the tone.

I come from the perfect family or at least that's what's so many people thought, looking from the outside in. It's a nice thought to think people don't care how you dress or how big your house is, whether your parents are good-looking, what kind of car you drive or what school you attend. I learned most people care, a lot. It's a different world for the privileged and it's not just the material perks. Beyond the illusions of perfection, dark secrets can hide. Total chaos can live undisturbed by social welfare, police and the laws imposed on everyone else. You see, money is a law unto itself. People can and do look away.

Money is power and in the hands of a psychopath, that level of power is as important to him as the need for one's own breath.

We were the original Instagram family before it even existed. Always dressed well, we lived in mansions, had the latest Mercedes or BMW, yachts that got bigger and bigger, gardeners, drivers, maids, house man, country clubs, boarding schools, holidays around the world, music lessons, dance lessons, tennis lessons, riding lessons, swimming lessons, language lessons, Burmese cats and an old English sheepdog. Mother taught us how to choose expensive wines, how to use the right formal cutlery, how to apply makeup professionally and how to pose for photos; seated sideways, legs crossed, head tilted, gentle smile, no teeth, perfect.

So, how did it all begin? That depends on how far back you want me to go. I think to really understand my story is to really understand my parents' stories, each as individuals, their histories, their values and their childhoods. So, I will begin by going back, all the way to my grandparents' stories, illustrating the context of that time, following the timeline all the way back to me. In doing this I hope to highlight patterns, generational inheritance, values, beliefs and secrets that shaped the narratives, choices, distortions, illusions, perceptions and one's identity along the way. The subconscious, somatic influences we all absorb through our senses—visual, audio, touch, taste and smell—as well as the beauty in observing the synchronicities, serendipity and how the right tools can cast new light into the shadows of our wounds.

I invite you to consider not only those things in our environment that are seen but also the influences from those things that are unseen. Energies that we spend years marinating in; that unless we learn to take control of can so easily morph into our beliefs, fears and values about ourselves and others. This bigger picture approach is the only true and honest way to get a full sense of how we come to understand, forgive, let go and even hold on with love to those things so abhorrently unforgivable to most. Trauma must be viewed with a wide lens to get the full angle.

I will also explore why, as children, we all held the family secrets, hiding them for so many years with the belief that to share them was our shame, our failing within the status of the system. Why every attempt to leave or call out the toxicity was punishable by the system that sustained its sickness.

That vicious cycle of the collective symbiotic relationship to our father, the master controller and to the enmeshed relationship of our parents. We each had our role, ascribed by our birth order and tested regularly, influencing our ranking. Threatened with emotional and financial abandonment and a regular dose of a firearm spraying bullets, just to remind us that his kind of rage wasn't the kind you called out if living was your priority.

If a child's point of reference begins with the very real and tried threat of death, then everything else pales in comparison. Mother bleeding from her head because Father pushed her became, 'Well, it's good he didn't hit her.' Not dying or being killed with the attempts or contemplated efforts to wipe us out became, 'I got to live.' I got to live will forever be the overriding victory of my childhood. At least from that, I can begin each day with a deep inhalation of enormous gratitude.

I will discuss the things I believe allows one to detach into adulthood and the steps needed to individualise. I will share some of the tools I know worked for me and thousands of my clients, with the hope and belief they can help you too. I will also share not just the historic past and its effect but also highlight what no one ever talks about in childhood abuse, the second wave. It is a time in your future when the resurgence of the past re-enters due to death, illness or a major event. Death, illness and stress stir the bottom of the pot, allowing all the old sediments to rise to the surface.

That second wave can be the tsunami you didn't see coming. Over time, the memories lessen, the pain fades and hope and trust settles in. Without forewarning, most will be unprepared for its wrath. For the remaining family members who didn't seek help or somehow couldn't keep their heads above the murky waters, this second wave can ignite as wounds flame and old family systems try once again to snuff you out.

The trauma and revictimisation rests in the forced re-entry into the same system that almost killed you. Regardless of how trained, healed or evolved you think you are, those old associations infantile you, forcing you back in time to the unresolved past. Navigating other's wounds that have festered in the dark, forced out of their slumber, there is no conclusion, no reconciliation, just the re-emergence of the perpetual chaos to nowhere. One is best to take cover.

Chapter Three
Just in Case Jewellery

My grandmother on my mother's side, Mary MacIntosh, was a petite, curly, dark-haired woman, 5ft 2 with piercing sky-blue eyes and porcelain skin. She married young and was widowed at age forty-eight. It was World War Two and she was just a simple dress shop owner in Scotland. After her husband's death, her business struggled; she was broke, hungry and afraid. I could only imagine the fear of so much uncertainty in a time when having no husband devalued a woman's position in life. Stoic and still very beautiful, she put on her red lipstick, dressed in her finest tweed, her only pair of shoes and went out to find a suitor. With all the soldiers around her, it wasn't long before she met a tall, lean and very handsome man named Stewart. She looked years younger than she was and her eyes easily seduced him. According to my grandmother, as told by my mother, it was mutual. Their love was intense, deep and progressed quickly. They had so much in common.

Stewart was an artist with works at the famous Tate Gallery. She was a pianist with a beautiful operatic voice and they delighted in each other's talents. Their affair began furiously with passion, excitement and hope to all her unrealised dreams, until she fell pregnant. Stewart agreed to marry my grandmother and professed nothing but love for her, except there was one minor problem, he was already married. My grandmother had no choice but to continue with the pregnancy. She moved to England to avoid the stigma and start life anew.

In 1933, my mother was born in London, England, Harriot Heather MacIntosh, an illegitimate child of an unwed mother and a child of an adulterous affair. My mother's birth wasn't registered at the time. I can't imagine Mary had any support, so likely birthed her alone at home. My grandmother did her best, but Stewart didn't follow through on their shared dreams. Perhaps he never intended to or maybe he measured the risks to his own family over the new one. I'll never know.

All the stories I have been told about my grandmother were shared with me on the rare occasions my mother found the courage to talk about her. When she did, her body tics, stuttering and uncontrollably tears were the worst I'd ever seen. Her whole body would spasm so violently it screamed its own story of the war she endured. Unfortunately, to my knowledge, my mother didn't have a photo of her mother. I did, however, find a sketching of her father, my grandfather, Stewart. Who drew it and how it came into her possession is unknown.

I found it amongst her photo albums given to me by my father after she died. The struggles of being an unwed mother with an illegitimate child in 1933 plagued my grandmother so much that my mother was placed in an orphanage by force at age one. My grandmother, swallowed by depression and grief, was then sent to a London asylum to spend the rest of her life. The asylum, Cane Hill, was one of the biggest at the time and housed almost two thousand patients. There were many reasons one might be

My mother's father, Stewart.

admitted; women still carried the reputation for a leaning toward neuroticism in the 1930s and certainly the societal values of what was acceptable would have heavily influenced my grandmother's plight. Widowed and pregnant at age forty-nine, the result of an adulterous affair with a married man, broke with a young child, I imagine it was deemed to be for her own good. The motto of the asylum at that time was 'Aversos compono animos'—I bring relief to troubled minds. Once in, very few ever got out.

Surrendered to the orphanage, my mother's life took a dramatic turn, altering her destiny and burdening her with the secrets she inherited. Those secrets hid in phobias, attachments, shame and fears but equally birthed an insatiable, wild and contagious humour and unflappable grit. Passed onto me at birth, those bittersweet, generational inheritances began the conflict within me of a mother I so deeply loved and admired and one that overburdened me with the role of therapist, mother and rescuer. My entire childhood role was to help her survive, literally and figuratively. My earliest memories of this began at age three.

It was years before when a random stranger bequest me with one of my greatest gifts, a message given in an innocuous, random chance meeting: 'Your mother's path is her own, you can't save her, don't even try as you'll just drown with her. Save yourself and from that you can always send her a lifeline.'

This is a picture of my mother aged five, standing outside her orphanage, worn out clothing, scraggly hair and a severely extended stomach, a result of starvation and malnutrition.

Harriot Heather MacIntosh, aged five.

Joan Crane.

She looked scruffy as a child however she inherited her mother's striking black hair and piercing blue eyes that contrasted against fine pale skin at a closer look. This was a good thing as it meant adoption was likely to be easier for her, or so she thought.

My mother was adopted around age five and, according to her, George and Nora Crane never did anything without researching things first. They most certainly were not looking for a child for the sake of taking on more responsibilities. The Cranes already had a daughter, Joan, who was born with severe health issues that involved multiple surgeries. She was their pride and joy. A blonde child, always dressed in the finest clothes and hair bows, she could do no wrong.

A second child named Nicholas died within a month. It was blamed on incompatibility to their bloods being Rhesus Negative and Rhesus positive. Having another biological child was not an option for the Cranes but they wanted a playmate for Joan. At first glance it all seemed rather lovely but as time passed and the story unfolded, my mother's true purpose was clearly revealed—she was an economic commodity. My mother learned quickly that being a ward of the state until age twenty-one came with financial benefits.

My mother arrived at her new countryside home in Sussex, England. It was a farm with a goat named Woggles, a Samoyed dog called Santa and three pigs; Narama, Farida and Fourouk, who to her horror was killed and eaten that night. She had never seen animals before but was impacted by that night and she quickly grew to love them dearly.

My mother was instructed to call the Cranes 'Auntie' and 'Uncle' and was told from now on she would be referred to as Heather. Heather Harriot MacIntosh. She loved her name as she learned Heather means a scruffy bush that can survive anywhere.

The house my mother grew up in was built in the 14th century. Made of flint stone, it was very cold and draughty. The only amenities were a cold water tap and a small brick oven. No electricity, no bathrooms and no hot water. There was a large bowl set on concrete in the corner of the kitchen, under which a fire was lit. Water was boiled to wash the clothes, sheets and towels. In the corner was a large stick used to transfer hot washes

My mother 'Heather' arrives at the farm

into cold water rinses. That stick was used to beat my mother often, one of many abuses she endured. The toilet was outside in an old dark shed often riddled with spiders. Toilet paper was yesterday's newspaper.

There was a long narrow room in the house that faced north. It had large hooks for cured meats, preserved eggs, sacks of potatoes and an endless array of jams, jellies and chutneys. It was the war years and my mother ate anything she was given—pigeon pie, rabbit stew, whale meat, tripe, stuffed heart and beef tongue.

My mother kept these staples in her fridge until the day she died. I called it 'the biology lab'.

The small village only had six children and Joan was the leader of the group. She wouldn't allow my mother to play with the others as she was illegitimate. At age six, Mum was given a hand mirror; it was the first and only gift she ever received as a child. It was given to her for her vocal talents by the local music teacher, Mrs Bromley Martin. She cherished it. Joan, ever jealous, smashed the mirror, breaking it into pieces. Mum went into Joan's room, took her favourite china doll, Esmeralda, and promptly smashed it on the ground. The large stick was used on my mum's backside so violently that day she couldn't sit on her bike when riding to school. She had only just learned to ride an old bike a few months earlier. It was gifted to her because Joan got a new one. Auntie taught her to ride the bike and sent her on an errand down the steepest hill in the village. She was to deliver tomatoes to a neighbour.

'Now Heather, whatever you do, don't you dare bruise those tomatoes,' Auntie teased.

Heather soon realised when picking up speed going down that steep hill that she didn't know how to stop the bike. Auntie had forgotten to teach her how to use the brakes. Hearing of the accident, Auntie scornfully said, 'I thought I told you not to bruise the tomatoes.' Mum crashed so hard, both her legs were fractured and she was bedridden for weeks. It was during her time recovering in bed at home, a social worker visited to check up on how she was doing. Mum told the social worker about the beatings and how she came to break her legs. The Cranes were given a stern warning but as the social worker only visited once a year, they simply ensured they would beat the idea of telling lies out of mum's mind once and for all. She never spoke to the social worker again.

While still resting in bed healing, she heard a man's voice calling her old name 'Harriot' from outside. The only other person at home was Auntie who suddenly appeared in her room. She gagged her mouth with her hand and told her, 'Not one word.' The man stayed for what seemed like forever but it was likely just minutes. The man was her father. It was the one and only time in her entire life she had a chance to meet him. She desperately clung on to the sound of his voice for years. Of all the abuses she ever endured, that haunted her the most.

My mother always wanted to learn how to swim with the other children in the village who often went to the river during the warmer months. Auntie, by now known for her harsh and abusive style in teaching new things, took her to the river herself. Without a word she got Mum to the edge and pushed her in. Mum struggled to get out, her head forced under the water while a snapping turtle was chasing behind her. This experience became the source of her greatest phobia, a severe claustrophobic response to anything touching her head, especially water.

As much as this was a very bad experience, fortunately life intercepted and she got a break. You see, when my mother turned seven, she was sent away to Auntie's parents as punishment for upsetting Joan once again. It seems Joan was cutting my mother's hair with the gardening shears when she cut the top of her ear off. Joan of course blamed her for moving, so in a fit of rage she sent Mum to the country to stay with her parents. Mum absolutely loved Auntie's parents. She spent her happiest years with them and even called them Grandpa and Grandma. My mother often spoke with excitement and laughter about how this punishment ended up being one of the most cherished times of her life. She was both loved and the centre of attention. Grandpa built a special cart that she could tie to the dogs and get pulled all around the garden.

She went to a new school and had lots of friends. She was and felt loved. It was the first time for so many things: first hot bath, first signs of kindness, first loving meals and the first time she felt safe.

Mum's grandparents made an application to adopt her, however, it was denied on the grounds they were too old. Learning of her angelic behaviour and missing out on the stipend of payments, Auntie Crane came back for her. On the first night of her return, Auntie served her a large piece of congealed pig fat. Refusing to eat it, Auntie picked up the plate and smashed it on Mum's head, saying that she would be sent back to the orphanage with bread and water. My mother picked up the piece of fat now on the floor and swallowed it in one large gulp.

Starved or rationed her entire life, by age twelve Mum had developed a problem with food and began stealing it. She couldn't get enough cold roast potatoes so she even began eating the local plants. Buttercup leaves have a slight tangy mustard flavour and sorrel a somewhat sharp and tart taste. Her favourite was hawthorn leaves, an almost nutty spinach flavour. Auntie, discovering what she was doing, said, 'Since you prefer plants, go pick your dinner tonight.' Mum went into the garden and picked a few herbs then discovered these beautiful tomatoes. She started eating them and as they tasted so good, she ate the vine clean.

What she didn't know was Uncle had developed a crossbreed named 'Plumpton King' and was planning to enter them in the upcoming horticultural show. Auntie grabbed her and dragged her into the outhouse, ripping out a large handful of hair in the process. She screamed and Auntie shoved a big black spider into her mouth and cupped her hand tightly over her face to keep it in. This was the beginning of her spider phobia that lasted her entire life.

Nora Crane, 'Auntie', was excelling as a lavish chef known for her exquisite displays of food. Her dinner and cocktail parties became famous within Sussex. As a result of her talents, Uncle, Auntie, Joan and Mum all moved to a cottage down the road from Major Shand and Lady Shand.

Uncle was hired as their gardener and Auntie as their cook. This was the last place my mother lived with the Cranes. I always wondered why even there under the watchful eye of such aristocratic people, my mother was still abused. Hot oil from a roast in the oven was 'accidently' poured over her legs as many other abuses continued. Why didn't anyone ever notice?

One good story did arise from her time there, however. On her 16th birthday, she received a gift from the Shands, allegedly from Prince (now King) Charles on behalf of his mother, Elizabeth II. It was a brooch with matching earrings, gold with peach stones and diamonds. My mother kept that wrapped in velvet her entire life. She kept it in case of an emergency, if she was starving, needed help at university, needed to leave my father or needed to save one of her children financially. She always knew she could cash in this magnificent set of fine jewellery. It served

My mother's just-in-case jewellery.

as her lifeline. No matter how bad things became, her just-in-case jewellery never had to be sold. Somehow that emotional insurance was just enough to keep her feeling safe. She believed this jewellery had her back.

It is in my safekeeping now, held sacred for the story it keeps. It would be over 75 years old now. It is amazing what our beliefs do for us, one way or another. It was decades later, towards the end of her life, when she finally showed it to my father. He burst out laughing. 'Oh, for Christ's sake Heather, it's fake, it's not worth a penny.'

On her deathbed, my mother placed her just-in-case jewellery in my hand and said with a smile, 'It's priceless!' Just thinking it was worth so much gave her the courage to push through. It held her up for most of her life and she cherished it. She was so grateful for how it served her. It's one of my most treasured pieces now too!

In her final years of school, my mother became quite rebellious. During an English lesson her teacher said, 'Watch the board,' so she walked up to the board and planted her nose, watching it intently. The class roared with laughter and that became her cue for more. Over six months she got seven detentions; an expulsion was eight. So, for the rest of the year her teacher gave her quarter detentions and she 'volunteered' for everything from selling raffles tickets to cleaning the church.

She was highly intelligent, fiercely funny, very musically talented and resilient. It is those skills that helped her and everyone from her teacher to the psychologist she was forced to see in her late teens recommended she go on to university. She sat the exams for university and auditioned for the Glyndebourne Opera House Choir, she was accepted in both. She enrolled in a degree program to become an occupational therapist. It included room and board, with soup with bread rolls for lunch. She had next to no money so would steal several bread rolls to cover her for dinner and breakfast. To earn extra money, she stood on a milk crate and sang for the soldiers. She was very petite at 5ft 3 and 45 kilograms wet.

Beautiful, with short, cropped hair, soldiers gathered around her like bees to honey. My mother had many creative talents and earned money for wealthy women sewing their dresses and weaving their basketry chairs. I remember her telling me one of the dresses was size twenty-two and had plastic fruit all over it. As my mother was a size four, she had to skilfully cut and tailor the dress—and of course, remove all the fruit. The result, according to my mother, was a very sophisticated and elegant dress.

She had two boyfriends during her time at university. The first was tall, Black, incredibly intelligent and musically gifted. She loved smoking cigarettes, drinking red wine and singing while he played piano. She loved him deeply and he proposed to her. She regretted her refusal but said she was too afraid of all the controversy at those times. She was already a controversy in her own right and couldn't bear any more stigma.

Her second boyfriend was tall and lanky with dark hair, he was an English lad who was sweet and funny. He adored my mother. Something happened to him, I am not sure what, I presumed he died as she became very upset and cried every time she spoke of him.

She chose the four-year course at university because it was the perfect combination of psychiatry and human behavioural studies. In addition to learning the complete study of anatomy, my mother had to produce finished articles of every craft to absolute perfection. She learned how to set up a box loom, create tapestries and rugs, spinning, dying and weaving yards of 45 inches wide, a tartan material with an even weave and straight edges.

The psychiatry side invited learning every symptom of every mental illness from the schools of thought: Freud, Jung, Adler, The Behaviorists, B.F. Skinner and emotional development or lack of. She trained in five hospitals. Friern Hospital (formerly Colney Hatch Lunatic Asylum) was the oldest psychiatric hospital in London (1851 to 1993). It had a strong smell when entering so my mother used to dab perfume above her lip just to get through her day. Formaldehyde was used to calm the patients and they still performed lobotomies, often reducing the patients to a vegetated state.

Friern opened up the back of the hospital so my mother and another student could work with male patients who had not had any visitors from the outside, apart from doctors and nurses, in over 30 years. Mum remembered every patient she ever had in all five hospitals.

There was a hospital she visited that proved to be the most devastating, as there was a small woman there with short, curly black hair, glass-white skin and the most piercing blue eyes. My mother told me it was her final day as a student when by chance she saw this woman. She always knew one day her fate would catch up to her and that she would have to face it. She walked into the ward and found this woman wild and clawing her tray like an animal. She knew at once who she was, subconsciously she was always on the lookout for her. She verified her name on the charts. It was her mother, my grandmother.

Meeting for the first time since their separation at age one, my mother's heart was pounding in her chest. She had only ever seen photos of her and didn't expect her to look so startling.

'Stop acting like an animal!' my mother shouted.

Her mother stopped immediately. She was mostly nonverbal but somehow seemed aware, if only for a few moments. Now, seated in front of a dressing table with a mirror, comb and hairbrush on display, my mother said, 'You have such lovely hair, do you mind if I touch it?' Very slowly, she brushed her mother's hair with long, gentle strokes. She even arranged it in several different ways.

She told her mother an imaginary story of a friend's birthday party, a monologue to introduce the month, the day and the year. Knowing her mother was a talented singer, she said, 'You know, I bet you're an amazing singer.' Her mother hummed softly throughout the rest of her visit. The bell rang, signifying the end of the session. My mother said, 'I don't know if I will see you ever again, but I wish you well' and gave her a big hug. Of course, the rules were no contact, certainly no hugs, but my mother knew that in this moment there was an allowance to break the rules.

My mother only told this story to me a few times in her entire life. The wounds of PTSD caused her words to stutter, her body to shake and her to cry uncontrollably. There could never be any more discussion when that happened and so it often just left the full story frayed at the edges of any real conclusion.

She left the hospital training with much deeper views of the real cause and effects of mental health issues and illnesses. One of the psychiatrists asked her, 'Well young lady, what do you think of your time here?'

'I find it very confusing there are people who shouldn't be here, by the same token I see people on the outside who I think should be here,' she replied.

'The line between sanity and insanity can be a very fine line often dictated by what society defines as reasonable or acceptable behaviour,' he said.

My mother understood that all too well as her beautiful, creative and passionate mother was sanctioned unreasonable by her love affair and illegitimate child. A generational inheritance, as I too feel incensed upon the societal sanctions against all women to this day for the oppressions of their own beautiful, free, powerful, innate wild.

Mum graduated with Honors and worked in England for a group of hospitals as a registered occupational therapist in the early 1950s. Years later, now married and living in Canada, my mother flew back to London and attended a student reunion. While there, a final year student came up to her and said, 'Are you the student at Friern called Mop-Head?'

'Yes,' she said.

'Thank God I found you. I have a message from that female patient with the beautiful voice and short black hair. She said I was unable to respond to you at the time but I want you to know that I remembered every word and action that day.'

It opened up the hope and excitement of perhaps reconnecting with her mother one day.

My mother met my father in Calgary, Alberta, Canada. It was around 1957 when on the spur of the moment she decided to accept the invite from her good friend Shirley to leave England for good. Why she left such a great position at the hospitals and her boyfriend at the time was uncertain. Ready for fun and adventure, she hurriedly organised her passport and a copy of her birth certificate.

At the registry of births death and marriages, a young man served my mother. When he saw her birth certificate marked illegitimate he promptly removed it with a wink of support. In fact, he went even further and obtained a birth certificate that named two complete strangers as her birth parents. My mother told me she flirted with the young man and requested he did this for her, as she needed documentation to migrate and wanted to be treated with respect, like a child born into marriage. The young man complied. I have the falsified documents in safekeeping as my mother always kept it. That gesture gave her the new start she was so longing for.

Shirley and my mother were only in Canada a few days when Shirley's ex-boyfriend, an English ex-pat named Phillip William Rolfe, organised a catch-up dinner. Drinks flowing, Phillip was extremely charming and took an instant liking to my mother. She said he was arrogant and intense and the first man she felt she could never say no to. She felt a chemical reaction, a combination of exhilaration and fear. They married ten days later. I always wondered, why the rush? My mother said on her wedding night she felt complete regret as she thought, 'Oh God, what have I done?'

Chapter Four
The Red Ants and the Black Ants

P hillip was the youngest of four children born to Algernon
and Winifred in London, England, in 1928. Algernon was
a tall, lean man who worked as a headmaster of a formal boys
grammar school, as well as serving at many levels in a military
career. In fact, his entire family, except for Phillip, all had active
roles in the military, as acting diplomats and in various careers
in politics. Algernon openly favoured his first-born son Ian,
often referring to him as the prodigal son. Ian was very good-
looking, tall, lean, stoic and intelligent but most importantly,
he followed his father's military pursuits. The two girls,
Shirley and Patsy, were equally photographed in military attire
and often proudly joined by their father. Both girls married
educated, successful military men, much to the approving eye of
their father who lavished very costly weddings on both.

Algernon moved his young family to Australia to join the
many relatives already living there, as he had lived there as a
farmhand from the age of sixteen to his early twenties. It was
in Australia where my grandfather began his military career;
first, joining the AIF and then the Army. Ian, Shirley and Patsy
were all born in Australia. Winifred, however, demanded they
return to England years later. She said the heat was simply
uninhabitable and, according to my father, she was very

persuasive. She was a stern woman who had a staunch coldness to her and kept her home constantly draughty, an irony to her natural character. That coldness formulated a deep concept of all women and their value in my father's mind, as Winifred directed a lot of that frost toward him. He was the child who carried the burdens of the family.

My father wasn't interested in following the rules and was acting out from a young age with bursts of anger. His parents' inability in those times to recognise and or diagnose attention deficit disorder or obsessive-compulsive disorder likely added to what became a Cluster B personality disorder (Psychopathy) later in life. The beginning staples were there at a young age, ready to flame into something more sinister—all it needed was a match. My father's earliest stories were always about the red ants and the black ants. He was five when he would gather red ants and black ants and pit them against each other. He found it amusing, inciting a battle while he stood back and watched the carnage. Divide and conquer was an innate skill he loved to practise.

He often spoke of how much he hated his sisters rousing him from his bed once asleep. Rotating him from bed to bed and using him as a bed warmer to stave off the starkness of the cold sheets upset him greatly. Seemingly an innocuous act, I wondered why he was so bothered by it until he told my brother and me about the reform school his mother insisted he go to. His grades were slipping, his motivation waned and he just wasn't behaving. Whether he stole or committed any crime is unknown, but he was still sent to reform school.

In the United Kingdom and its colonies, reform schools were set up from 1854 onwards for youngsters who were convicted of a crime as an alternative to an adult prison. Stealing a pair of shoes would be enough to commit you for several years. Indications for admittance could also be:

- Severe mood swings
- Disinterest in hobbies and friends
- Defiance
- Lack of motivation
- A dramatic drop in grades
- Resistance to authority
- Intense emotional outburst
- Increased aggression
- Stealing
- Skipping school
- Bullying

There was a very high rate of sexual exploitation and molestation incited by the older juvenile offenders, causing most children to become worse when they were released. My brother told me that our father admitted he had been sexually abused. There lies the beginning of everything.

SECRET #2

Father was sent away to reform school where conditions were strict, punishments were severe and sexual abuse was rampant.

He had secrets, my father. The kind that stays stagnant, forced down by shame and fear, festering into rage. Over the years he tried to drown it with alcohol, but nothing could hold that beast down. Over time, the beast grew bigger as it simply fed off those cold, damp dungeon walls of his mind. Kept hidden, the darker triads of his personality had a secret place to thrive. It buried with it deep wounds of low self-worth and a constant insatiable need to prove he was better. Contrasted by chronic addictions and an insatiable quest to fuck every woman he met, regardless of his marital status, his inevitable ageing or declining health.

As a child, he seemed fond of his sister Patsy and described her as gentle and kind, but he disliked Shirley, describing her as stern, like his mother. Shirley teased him a lot and if tested he would always find a way to seek revenge, even if it took years. Revenge in the case of Shirley was paying her large sums of money in her older years whilst reminding her of how humiliating that was and that it resulted from her own incompetence. A strong, highly successful woman with a career in the military and politics for most of her life, that would have been very castrating to her sense of dignity. That was its power.

Algernon brought the family back from Australia to Essex, England, to the family farm estate. It was grand and opulent, a proper English manor, with many rooms, topiary gardens and an enormous shed. One would think it's the kind of home any child would want to live in forever and yet my father left at the age of fourteen. His brother Ian was soaring in his military career, becoming Lieutenant in his twenties. Enlisted in the Australian Airforce, he bravely followed in his father's footsteps. My father, however, had no voice, no foothold and no chance of redeeming himself of any value in his parents' eyes. He told me years later he didn't need anyone; no family, no friends, he didn't feel those emotions other's felt and he was fine on his own, so he left on that sentiment. It is likely his father Algernon, his mother Winifred, his sister Shirley and the boys reform school instigated those early issues that drove him to leave, significantly altering his life and the life of my family forever. A flower in a hostile environment will surely turn to weed.

So, at age fourteen, he left home. According to my father, he lied and enlisted himself into the Italian Army. As my understanding is the Italian Army didn't recruit foreigners, I suspect he simply went to Italy and offered his services in exchange for room and board. His job was to drive the small boat off the south coast of Italy to an island close by and bring the prostitutes over for the army men. My father said one beautiful Italian prostitute was his first love. He smoked two packs of cigarettes a day, drank regularly and slept with many of the prostitutes. He often spoke of how much he enjoyed his time there.

Three years later he received a telegram from his father saying his brother Ian was dead. At the tender age of twenty-four, Lieutenant Ian David Rolfe, fighting the war in Japan for the Australian Air Force, crashed and became a POW. The Japanese prisoner of war camps that were notorious for inflicting insidious tortures. Starved, beaten and severely malnourished, Ian was part of the death march.

I imagine my grandfather viewing images of these POWs with a full spectrum of engaged senses, he would know what they were thinking, feeling and experiencing in that moment. The mental anguish of ruminating thoughts and feelings, his beloved son amongst these men.

Ian died in an unimaginable torture. Inconceivable to me, however, my military grandfather knew exactly what happened to his son in detail, every torture, every terrorising fear, the concept of starving and dying alone at age twenty-four, his prodigal son. Did he have guilt? Was his rage masked by grief and did a part of Algernon die too? How would an English gentleman, a school headmaster, an army Lieutenant cope? How did Winifred cope? A housewife, she spent countless days and months at home with her youngest son while the rest of the family committed to their military training and duties. At home alone with the son she disliked—he was not athletic, was seemingly disinterested in anything and had outbursts of anger and disruptions so he did not measure up to the family standard. She often told my father, 'Children are to be seen, not heard.' After all, her only job was to ensure the children did as they were told—and he never did. He was stubborn, smart, clever and angry with an anger that festered deep in the bowels of his soul. It was a rage that had tentacles that could snuff the life out of anyone who dared confront his behaviour. It was not an era when a parent might consider investigating why their child acted out in such rage. It was just considered a blithe on Phillip's character, impudent and deliberate.

After Ian's death, my father went home to pay his condolences, however, he was told it should have been him. Why wasn't he the one who died? He was the useless one, the disobedient one. He was reminded by Shirley, Winifred and Algernon that Ian was more of a man, better looking, braver and therefore my father could never measure up to him and that the real son died. I suppose someone had to absorb the pain of the family and he had unwittingly volunteered to be the scapegoat from an early age. Over time he simply believed he deserved it and acted the part. The saying 'sticks and stones can break your bones, but words will never hurt you' is wrong. Words change you, your mind, your values, your identity, your self-worth; words can flick that switch. Words can kill. You can't always tell when a soul has died as it's on the inside.

I wonder in the mist of the family's insurmountable grief if they ever considered how my father was feeling. Always a staunch anti-war, anti-military child, Ian's torture and death confirmed his deepest fears. Yet he was somehow left to carry the responsibility of this great burden on the family. He was also convinced he had to and there birthed a lifelong insatiable quest to prove his worth.

There is an eleven-year gap between my father's time in Italy and his arrival in Canada at age twenty-five—long enough to have a wife and or children, a more likely possibility knowing my father, but one we shall never know for certain.

He arrived in Quebec, Canada, by ship. He would often tell me stories of how he scouted young women still living at home and charmed their fathers into offering him free room and board with the prospects of their daughters marrying this fine, English man. He knew how to charm and often laughed at how most of the fathers threw in a car to up the ante of the deal.

My father ended up in Edmonton, Alberta, the complete opposite end of Canada, staying with many, many women and their families along the way. Once there, it was only days before he got a message from an old English girlfriend he met years earlier in Italy, with the same name as one of his sisters, Shirley.

Shirley arranged a dinner and told him she had newly arrived from London with her best friend Heather whom he absolutely had to meet.

He arrived looking very handsome, meticulously dressed and was wildly charming. My father always had an obsessive determination for having and being the best. He had a commanding confidence, was an astute observer and calculated every move he made as if he was playing a game of chess. At first glance of my mother, a very petite, graceful version of Audrey Hepburn with cropped black hair, red lipstick and piercing blue eyes, he declared checkmate.

She was funny, sexy and highly intelligent with a job lined up as head therapist at a psychiatric hospital. She was outwardly confident. In fact, she lit up the room with this energy that was vibrant and palpable. I remember my mother telling me he was the first man she felt she would never be able to say no to, he wouldn't let her. She found that intriguingly sexy at that time. It's amazing what candlelight, good wine and hidden wounds can filter.

I believe theirs was a meeting of the unconscious wounds. It is said that elevated chemical response that makes you feel an overwhelming rush is not love after all but your wounds being triggered. If only they knew about trauma bonding then. My mother's wounds fell for a man who instantly overpowered her and made her feel she would be so lucky to have him and that keeping him would always be her responsibility, no matter what he did. My father's wounds smelt the fears of abandonment despite her beauty and hard-earned merits. A serious and committed task for an orphan who held tight to the fears of abandonment and loss, he knew she would be blinded by the tentacles he threw her, instead viewing them as a lifeline of which she would never, could ever, let go. That is the power of such a pairing.

My father overcompensated his hidden, wounded, insecure inner child with excessive drinking, smoking, gambling, spending, flirting and impulsive behaviours. However, he wore tweed jackets, linen pants, leather shoes, a gold Rolex, gold money clip, gold lighter and he always drove an expensive sports car. He mastered the art of deflection. Splashed generously in Old Spice cologne, clean shaven, thick, blonde wavy hair and a strong chin that highlighted his English, Nordic and Germanic lineage, he knew his power.

My father proposed to my mother days later and she accepted. He mumbled something about a business trip and not leaving without her. He chose my mother both for her incredible grace, intellect and beauty but more importantly because of her history of being orphaned and having no family. He hedged his bets she would remain loyal, regardless of what he did, as she had an insatiable need to be loved, to have a family and to never be starved or abandoned again. Of all the bets he made, this was his greatest win as my mother stayed with him for fifty-eight years.

Chapter Five
Mum, Man Unknown

A quick business trip for my father to America, his new fiancé in tow, they got married by registrations in the courthouse of Ohio. I imagine my father thinking, 'Nothing like killing two birds with one stone'. They settled in Edmonton, Alberta as my mother had secured a job as an occupational therapist in a prominent mental health hospital. She was the main financial breadwinner as he was trying to find financial backers for a reinsurance company he was formulating. Having worked in insurance companies already, he saw his potential for large, generated wealth from reinsurance (when one insurance company purchases protection from another insurance company to reduce its exposure to risk).

They lived in a small house but were well known for their lavish cocktail parties with elaborate spreads. My mother always dressed formally in tight pencil shirts, V-neck jumpers or tailored blouses, low-heeled pumps, pearls and strong French perfume dabbed on her wrists and neck ever sparingly. My father, not one to be outdone, was equally dressed in linen pants, cashmere blazers and crisp, well-ironed cotton shirts with a coordinated tie, leather shoes and socks with monogrammed initials.

A well-stocked bar was always visible with crystal tumbler glasses for aged whiskey, vodka or gin. Except for a few personally selected pieces, most of my mother and father's clothes were secretly sourced from Op shops. Having learned the art of the perfect hunt in London, my mother was a master at finding the best quality, even designer clothes, at the cheapest price. The size never mattered as she was skilled at sewing and could tailor-fit anything within minutes on her Singer machine.

Mother received a letter from Dorothy Pullinger, the children's liaison officer for the London Country Council, that included a letter from the attending physician at Cane Hospital, who was attending to her mother. It seemed after her visit her mother had an incredible full recovery and was now there on a volunteer basis and working in several areas of the hospital. He requested that she visit more often as it would be extremely good for her mother and for my mother also. She asked my father for permission as it was the 1950s and she had the binds of her past that leant toward submission; it was a firm no, 'Over my dead body' response. My mother never saw her mother again.

Just seven months after getting married, my mother became pregnant with their first child, Heidi, born in February 1957. She was a nervous first-time mother, insisting everything be ritually cleaned in Dettol, including my father before holding Heidi. This soon became a catastrophic decision, however, as only two months later, on their first outing to a grocery store, Heidi caught meningitis. Hospitalised for several months, she almost died.

It was at this time my father's behaviour really worsened. Out late, arriving home drunk most nights, he offered no explanation except to say, 'None of your business'. Mother spent most of her time at work or socialising with her colleagues. He would often start the argument that became one of two highly charged arguments they had in their fifty-eight years of marriage. He would accuse her of having an affair and, therefore, Heidi being illegitimate. My siblings all heard these arguments but as they were drowning in copious amounts of alcohol, we became desensitised to it.

Over the years Heidi grew and grew, far surpassing all of us in height. She reached 5ft 11¾ by age twelve while the rest of us ranged between 5ft 6 to 5ft 10. Chris and I had fair, wavy, hair, Keily; had slightly reddish hair and Heidi had darker hair with slightly different features. None of the siblings gave it another thought until years later. Except for Keily, who often teased Heidi that her real father was Native Indian because of her long dark hair, she nicknamed her Pocahontas.

As teens we all revisited the thought it might be true. Perhaps Heidi did have a different father. By that time our parents had revealed so many twists and turns in their affairs, lies, secrets and dysfunctions, we erred on believing in more scandal than not. Who did what first was no more enticing than what came first, the chicken or the egg. It's a futile discussion as one could argue it infinitely. However, one can be certain that history predicates the future.

It was years later, after the deaths of my parents, that I received a large box of family photos from our deceased estate lawyer. Going through them I found a photo of my mother sitting

Photo of Mum with an unknown man.

on a bench with a man's arm wrapped around her. On the back
was written: 'Unknown man with Mum?'

My heart sank. That argument echoed in my head and
challenged me with the question, 'What if it's true?' The writing
was likely my sister Keily's. Heidi confirmed it wasn't hers and
I compared it to letters from Keily that I had in my possession.
She had obviously done some hunting. A second picture was able
to match that hand and showed this tall, dark-haired, lanky man
draped around my mother in an adoring pose.

Mum with an unknown man and two little girls.
Was he Heidi's father?

SECRET # 3

Mum possibly had an affair with a married man while also married to my father. Was he her boyfriend from England? Was she planning to leave with him?

Heidi was raised with all the good, the bad and the ugly of our father. Whether she is biologically my sister, in half or full, is irrelevant to me. She is my sister. It might explain, however,

My sister Heidi. Is the unknown man her biological father?

why we are at opposite ends of the spectrum in personality. These photos aren't conclusive in resolving the secret, but they surely raise the possibilities. Heidi said, 'At least my father adored me.' I concurred and smiled warmly at that thought too.

Heidi was an only child for the first three years. My father wanted to work in a company he found in Winnipeg, Manitoba, as he saw it leading him closer to the networking he needed to build his own company one day. So, the family moved from Calgary to Winnipeg into a large white house. They bought a dog to keep Heidi company, as by this time Heidi was talking to her imaginary friend, Peter. Peter was a regular at all meals, requiring a knife, fork and a plate on which to eat his meals at Heidi's insistence.

Keily was born next in December 1960. Heidi was thrilled to have a sibling and was often photographed with Keily in her arms. Light-haired with specs of red and a generous sprinkle of freckles across her face, Keily looked very much like a fairer version of our mother. Both girls were meticulously dressed in frilly frocks and tailored coats with pigtails or long hair. Heidi was given the job from the start of being responsible for Keily, a big task for a three-year-old. She was far too young to fully comprehend what was expected of her so a good thump on the back of the head and a 'Fucking idiot' or 'Stupid girl' was the beginning of my father's subconscious imprinting into who she would perceive herself to be. A deeply ingrained belief system I still see to this day at the core of my beautiful sister's tics and social discomforts.

My mother was often finding ways to leave my father, beginning only months after their marriage. She was such a competent, highly educated woman, yet she seemingly always felt her only way out was with a man. Having never met her own father, subconsciously my father replaced that figure of the rejecting, abandoning parent. Mother was either trying desperately hard to be the good girl and do as she was told or to replace him with a new daddy. She couldn't possibly bear to leave and find herself alone without a dad once more. That would be a greater death to her psyche than staying in abuse. My father knew that. He chose well.

My father had been acting strangely for some time with the next-door neighbour, a woman named Sharon. Sharon was married and had several children of her own. She was highly flirtatious and what my mother called 'too familiar' with my father. My father was, of course, always inappropriately flirtatious with all women and because he 'never met a woman he didn't want to fuck', had the affair with Sharon. My parents argued about this affair and my mother's alleged affair my entire childhood and it was their biggest drunken argument until their deaths. The argument between my parents developed the day my mother found out Sharon was exactly the same month into her pregnancy as my mother. Both carrying a son, my mother was shocked when Sharon declared her soon-to-be-born son would be named Christopher, the same name my mother picked out for her soon-to-be-born son—a name only my father knew she had chosen. Both Christophers were born in July 1962, just days apart.

SECRET #4

My father had an illegitimate son, also named Christopher, with Sharon. A son he stayed in touch with for most of his life and even supported financially.

My mother's son, my brother, also named Christopher, had hair so fair it was almost white, stunning blue eyes, full pouty lips and was over 10 lbs. at birth, albeit breech. Christopher was my father's prodigal son. Having to stop working after the birth of Heidi, my mother spent her days knitting jumpers, sewing gonk dolls or Raggedy Anns, cooking, cleaning, making jewellery called 'leather by Heather', writing a weekly news article in the local paper and selling Tupperware. Very thin and always busy, she lived on fifteen cups of coffee a day, a housewife's equivalent to cocaine in the sixties. She also smoked a pack of cigarettes a day as being thin was what true wealth and elegance were supposed to look like. She allowed herself one meal a day and that was dinner, most often accompanied by a glass or two or three of aged port. My mother fell pregnant again two months after Christopher was born. She was incredibly ill from the onset and vomited everything she ingested.

Already devastated by the neighbour Sharon, trapped in a life she felt she had no choice but to stay in, she did something she held great guilt over her entire life. She purposely spent an entire day lifting very large couches and shifting them around the room. She did this repeatedly, pushing, lifting and even holding the large pieces of furniture until she felt sharp pains from the strain. It worked. She miscarried the baby she just couldn't carry at that time.

Pregnant with me only six months after she miscarried, I think it added to the incredible bond we carried from the beginning. Guilt and a chance to reclaim the baby she had lost, she often told me I reminded her that it just as easily could have been me and that thought was just too much to bear. Born a rather underweight baby, I think I scraped through the last of what my mother's body felt she could muster. I am so very, very grateful I somehow got through to this world and that in spite of her many foibles, she was my mum. With four children under seven, my mother had a right to be, feel and acknowledge she was overwhelmed.

In the sixties, airing your dirty laundry wasn't acceptable. You married and you got what you got. Longevity was the measurement of success, not growth. A good woman was measured by how much she could take, without letting her slip show. My mother was trained for that. Drinking and smoking, having affairs and keeping your chaos and dysfunction nicely swept under the carpet were the real measure of class and civility. Father always said, 'The English mastered the art of civility. Once you do that, anything goes, as long as its hidden and kept tidy.'

Chapter Six
Four Children Cross
the Highway, Three Return
Birth–age 4

I t's hard to know what stories you truly remember from your earliest years and those you've heard passed down from your parents or siblings. I can confidently say my memory can go back as far as age three. It's broken into sensory pieces of images, smells, specific words or sentences but also reactions from others who cued me into taking note, pressing pause and highlighting those imprinting moments. Many I saved for later, knowing one day I would review them with a keener, deeper understanding. After all, I was just a little girl.

It was a beautiful sunny day in Winnipeg, something you take note of when nine months of the year we experienced harsh weather. I was excited and wanted to go to the park. The problem with that, however, was you had to cross a large highway to get there. So, Mother arranged for Heidi to take Keily, Christopher and me for a play. I'm not sure why she didn't take us or what she had to do instead, but sure enough, Heidi took us all. This is where my memory fades and my mother's storytelling takes over. Laughing at how humorous it all was, she would recall how Heidi walked through the door a few hours later, all by herself.

'Heidi, where's Keily, Chris and Deirdre?'

'Oh, Keily is watching them.'

'OK,' replied Mum.

Thirty minutes later, Keily walked through the door all by herself.

'Keily, where's Chris and Deirdre?'

'Oh, Chris has her.'

'OK,' she replied.

A few minutes later, Chris walks through the door.

'Oh for Christ's sake, Christopher, where is Deirdre?'

'Heidi has her,' he said.

My mother was absolutely panicked so she poured a glass or two or three of sherry and waited for my father to come home that evening. My parents went to the police station and reported me missing. I was returned by the police twenty-four hours later. A woman had found me and taken me home, fed me, bathed me and put me to bed. She contacted the police the next day. I can hear my mother laughing as she told that story many, many times and my father chuckling in the background as they both found it so terribly funny. I have no memory of that experience, except being very confused they weren't guilt-ridden or burdened by their choices whenever they relayed the story. Perhaps it became humorous over time, as the relief I was safe allowed them to turn it into something lighter, to lessen its weight. Either way, lessening the seriousness seemed convenient at the time. They told the story but flipped the tone of the script.

I noticed that then, even though I couldn't articulate it quite in the way I felt it. I never thought anything about that story was even remotely funny. No matter how many times I pressed review,

Four Children Cross the Highway, Three Return

I was and still am aghast that we all were left under the care of Heidi to cross a busy highway and play in a park unattended. To further highlight the extraordinary lapse of good adulting or good parenting on behalf of my mother in her nonchalant manner, I was three, Chris was five, Keily was seven and Heidi was ten. Not only is it miraculous none of the children got hit by a car as they crossed the busy highway, but I was also taken. I was picked up by a stranger, who took me into her home. I got to live, again.

Just as quickly as that event was over, we were on a family holiday, starting with a visit to London to visit Grandma, Grandpa and their dog Bella. Grandpa named me Little Miss Green Pants because of my daily penchant for wearing stretchy green pants. Being the youngest and with my stark bowl haircut, I do believe fourth in line just got what they got. I didn't mind, I found Little Miss Green Pants endearing. My father had a knack for being so incredibly angry and distant, yet on holidays it was as if he was trying to make up for all the bad times he put us through. He was charming, generous and even occasionally picked me up for a photo or touched my head as if to pat a dog. We loved this version of our father; it sustained us throughout our entire lives and even to this day.

The irony of the devoted wounded child is that they will savour the breadcrumbs once starved long enough, as your tastebuds heighten the sensory memory. Over time, however, it became more and more confusing, until eventually, we all saw it as his pattern of control. Hot, cold, in, out, love, give, hate, withhold, punish, reward, punish, reward, divide and conquer. We discovered he was selective in how he allowed others to see him and he could control it as easily as a flick of a switch. Holidays were more exciting and adrenaline fuelled as love bombing created an enormous dollop of dopamine. That high is palpable to a child of abuse and becomes a feeling anchored deep into their psyche. It's a feeling that will be searched for later in life through love, sex, addictions, gambling, excess shopping or, for the few lucky ones, running, dancing, nature or travel. We were all encoded.

While still holidaying in England, we boarded one of the biggest cruise ships at the time, the Oriana, for a European sail. No expense was spared as we even had a hired nanny. I remember her well. She used to take me behind this enormous curtain and spank me repeatedly. I have no idea why she did that but I remember I didn't like it. That feeling of something not being right, that a rhythm was off, was with me from as early as age three. I remembered thinking she seemed a bit off and she had a bit of a problem. This is a fairly complex and self-assured way for a three-year-old to think but the memory has given me much insight as to why, somehow over the years, I survived.

I believe a little grit is an innate characteristic. I just got lucky in the DNA recipe of my parents; a genetic Russian roulette where one gets a little more sugar, one gets a little more salt and one gets a little more spice. I got a little extra spice. It was highlighted in another memory I had on the Oriana. It was Halloween and there was a homemade costume party for the children with prizes for first, second and third-place winners. My mother was the queen of homemade costumes. She was always creative and made the costumes we wore each year; one of us was a sure win.

I remember all these children lined up in rows waiting for their turn to walk up to the judges and stand quietly in front of them. We were prepared to behave as instructed and every child did as they were told, it was the times after all. Heidi was a Hawaiian hula dancer, Keily was a snowman, Christopher was a traffic light and I was a bunny. I was wearing my black ballet body suit, black ballet stockings, black ballet slippers, bunny ears, whiskers done in black mascara and had a big cotton tail. Each of my siblings went up before me as it was done according to age. I remember I panicked when my name was called. I was so focused on wanting to be the best bunny I could for myself, my siblings and my mum. So, with a deep breath, I immediately cuffed my hands like bunny paws and hopped to all the judges. I became the bunny and I won.

I love that little girl. I am so proud of how, regardless of what she endured in the shadows, she claimed her experience. But since I was still only three, I refused to eat anything on that entire cruise other than cream of wheat. I liked it warm, with a little cream floating at the top and a dollop of raspberry jam. That made me feel so, so blissfully happy that my mind felt like it was bathing in it.

Back home in Winnipeg, I don't remember much else about my young life except a few things, like my father always saying, 'Don't lick a metal pole in winter or your tongue will get stuck.' Keily did exactly that, of course she had to test the theory out. Four and a half years older than me, she was seven and a bit when she licked a metal pole in the depths of winter, just outside our house. My father rushed out with a kettle of very warm water and splashed it onto her tongue, releasing a very swollen and sore but nevertheless intact tongue.

I also remember a lot of conversations about ghosts beginning at this time. Our dog Max had died and my mother would often hear him scratching at the back kitchen door and open it to let him in. My mother was very open about hearing or seeing ghosts and all of us as children showed what she thought was an inheritance of the intuitive gifts passed down from our grandmother. These gifts of seeing, hearing and feeling through the intuitive were a common feature throughout my entire childhood.

We all spoke of the ghosts, shadows and whispers or the weird events throughout our lives. Mother always honoured and encouraged these conversations. Perhaps that's why she felt we could fend for ourselves. Or perhaps both my parents only knew having to fend for themselves, so they normalised that for us. Heidi was always playing, or doing art or eating her meals with Peter, her imaginary friend. That's what my father called it but my mother believed he was a true ghost; she also saw and heard him often. Peter was a blonde-haired child who appeared to be around the age of ten. Heidi loved him and remembered him from as early as two, although my mother noticed Heidi responding to him as a baby. Their friendship was a connected and enduring one, at least until she herself was aged ten.

Drunk and in a bad mood, which by now was all so common, our father sat down to dinner and we all joined him. Next to Heidi was an empty chair with a usual setting for Peter. Just as my mother placed the little plate of food in front of Peter's chair, my father stood up, grabbed the plate and threw it against the wall. He then abruptly sat on Peter and raged, 'Peter is dead. I sat on him and killed him.' Peter was never spoken of again.

Chapter Seven
The White House
Age 4–6

D ad found investors for his company RE/EX and moved the family to a two-storey, white house in North Vancouver. The house had a small back garden with a steep embankment that sloped down through a pine forest with ample thorny bushes. The ground floor had four bedrooms, one for each of us, a small living room, a laundry room and a door connected to the garage. The staircase to the top floor was next to my room, which scared me as I would often hear my father slam the door on his way in. His heavy footsteps always made him sound taller and bigger than he was, I think he liked it that way. Upstairs was my parents' bedroom, a living room, a kitchen and the bathroom we all shared.

There were many things I loved about this house. My bedroom wall was bubble-gum pink and I had a single wrought iron bed with a white laced bedspread, simple but very pretty. One wall was covered in Humpty Dumpty wallpaper. I felt sad for Humpty Dumpty but he reminded me not to be fragile like an egg as he hung precariously off a wall. I thought it best to keep my feet firmly on the ground and never lose my balance because all the king's horses and men couldn't put poor Humpty back together again. I found that so scary.

Metaphors always spoke loudly to my mind. A combination of my own innate system and the influence of my mother, who by this time was purposely imprinting me through my senses with anything and everything that created empowered resilience. Music, dance, metaphor, symbolism, words, phrases, rituals, art, she used everything in her toolbox to psychologically anchor me for survival. I think she resigned herself to her own fate, all the way back then, but made it her mission to save her children. She wanted to save us all, but somehow as the youngest and with our very close bond, she invested generously with me.

She was already in the battle of her life with my father, so she used her skills as an occupational therapist to prepare me for that war too. I remember the colour of her mustard jumper and the smell of her warmth and love as she cuddled me on her lap while drinking a cup of coffee. It was a ritual to just pause and hold me, her way of saying she loved me; she never could muster the words to say it out loud.

Sometimes we would lay on the lounge chairs outside on a sunny day, watching scattered clouds, scrying the shapes for meaning. One of the many forms of divination she subconsciously inherited from what she believed to be an innate, generational skill she saw in me. The meaning of the symbols was both subjective and based on the universal collective, like dream interpretation. Hearts meant love or what's at the heart of the matter. A book meant a lesson learned or a search for a deeper meaning. A bell meant a blessing or clearing a space for good energy and protection. A sun was positivity, great luck and abundance. A raven was a message from an ancestor. A bear was having or needing protection. A star was to wish upon a star and all will come true.

Scrying, also known by various names such as 'seeing' or 'peeping', is the practice of looking into a suitable medium in the hope of detecting significant messages or visions. The objective might be personal guidance, prophecy, revelation or inspiration, but down the ages, scrying in various forms also has been a means of divination or fortune-telling.

We would share our sightings and fill each other up with the supportive messages we received. It was all part of our language. I believe it was a language we both naturally saw, but it also gave us a lifeline to communicate when father was getting worse. Mother would also take me to the beach where we would spend hours picking beautiful shells we could later make a wind chime out of. Or we would walk through the forest, picking blackberries, finding wild herbs by the creek or just walking for hours without any sense of where we were going. She loved getting lost. I used to always ask her where we were going and she'd always say with a giggle, 'I have no bloody idea. Isn't that just marvellous my darling.' We were always in nature. I believe she was teaching me to face those fears or restraints life so often throws at us. She was wild, beautifully, naturally, powerfully wild. It was her strength, that one thing that kept her alive, kept her mind free, knowing no matter how many people tried to claim it or destroy it, she won. She always unapologetically owned her true, authentic, wild self.

I loved my mother more than any tangible words could ever describe. I will always cherish and honour her for saving my life and breathing that spark of hope, magic and light into my mind, down deep to the space within me that thrives. These moments filled me. It's an incredible, powerful thing to have those moments in life, where no words are needed and yet energy is felt, a bond so tightly connecting it's palpable. It's a love so transcendent it is shared in our breath, in our body and in everything we see. These moments last forever, these moments are eternal.

But then, there were those other days where Mother would whisper, 'He's getting worse'.

Heidi remembers that too and even said Mother told her several times, 'I think he's trying to kill me'. It was strange, as it was always just a whisper, passing in the hallways or whispered quickly as she said good night in our bedrooms. I think she knew we couldn't do anything but wanted us to know if she did get killed it was him.

Mother started taking me to psychics, gypsies and spiritual fairs. She thought I had a gift of seeing. The psychics all said I was very strong in my abilities and to keep encouraging me. My mother encouraged that spiritual, cultural inheritance of symbolism, metaphor and ritual my entire life. It is integrated and highlighted in the fusion of psychology I use and in my practice as a therapist. How could it not be? It is who I am. It is also at the core of my own healing journey and one I believe gave me tools, perspectives and choices unique to most interventions. When I reach back into the ancestral teachings of my Vikings and Celtic warrior lineage, it gives me leverage to battle any war.

Chris and Keily weren't as close to our mother as Heidi and I were. Father called Chris the prodigal son and Keily was Keepie, which seemingly meant nothing, but he said she was prettier, sweeter, lovelier and the favourite. Divide and conquer began when we were all very young. It didn't set us up to dislike each other, however, not when we were very young anyway, but it did create a mutual behaviour where we all thought we had to work harder for Father's love. Chris and Keily worked harder to get the extra cash, gifts and affirmations, Heidi and I worked harder just to get a breadcrumb of what he had left. I didn't really mind, as I loved my mother and felt comforted at least with that. Heidi felt the same, although on birthdays or at Christmas, it was hard not to feel the pinch of our father's very deliberate acts to divide us.

One Christmas, Chris and Keily both received a cheque for one thousand dollars while I got a cheque for one hundred dollars. I remember being so excited and happy my father gave me one hundred dollars. 'Oh, thank you Father, thank YOU.' I was truly happy for them, they were older and it seemed fair, they needed more clothes than me. But I also knew what it meant and felt sad realising that even on Christmas Day my father just wanted to hurt me. It was a sport to him. It did hurt me, but where my father got it wrong was that it was never about the value or amount of the money given, just the meaning he always ascribed to it. His intentions were what hurt. Knowing your father or anyone you love hurts you without provocation and when you're just a nice, young girl is painful. And I was a lovely, cheeky, soft-hearted girl.

Those feelings of confusion and hurt over our father's favouritism didn't last long however, as by the afternoon I just didn't think about it. We all learned to forget things like that. I was happy that Keily and Chris got money, I loved them. Besides, Mother made hot cross buns and there were no fights or drunken chaos. Today was a good day and I was happy with that. You see the mistake my father made was that he underestimated how much we all loved each other. We all experienced the abuse. We knew no one was more special, prettier or uglier, smarter or more stupid. We knew it was our father just trying to hurt us. Chris was always protecting me and Keily would make me tea and bake cookies and tell me how pretty I was. It was just money and as children, at least back then, we just loved each other.

Chris struggled to sleep at night and was wetting his bed regularly. An avid reader he started devouring books. He had an extensive Hardy Boys collection and often read until two or three in the morning. My parents said he wet his bed because he drank too much tea and stayed up too late. We all knew he was struggling with the fights, drinking and chaos in the home. We were all showing signs of this outwardly in some form. I ate too many cookies, was chubby and talked too much; Chris wet his bed, struggled to sleep at night and read ferociously; Heidi was reclusive and introverted, escaping into her art; and Keily had her animals and was very, very shy.

Heidi was eleven when we moved to the white house, Keily was eight, Chris was six and I was four. I remember walking up those stairs one night as I was hungry and wanted a snack. I was sitting in Heidi's room with Keily and Chris and I stood up and announced what I was doing. They all tried to convince me not to go upstairs. I couldn't understand why not and being hungry I marched into the kitchen. I was standing in the hue of the light from the opened fridge door when my father suddenly appeared.

'Deirdre, WHAT ARE YOU DOING?' he said with his plumb-in-the-mouth English accent.

'Nothing, I'm getting a snack.'

'Don't you realise you are FAT? Do you hear me? YOU ARE FAT.'

I didn't understand what that meant but it sounded bad and my subconscious mind imprinted that message, having a lasting impression on my relationship with weight and food my entire life. For years I thought I was fat. My father told me I was. As I grew, I ebbed and flowed in my weight depending on the stability of my emotions and the depths of happiness in my life. Weight has always been my body's barometer, the truth of how I am a measurement of feeling lost or found, abandoned or loved, threatened or safe.

It wasn't until years later, as an adult, I reviewed the photos of my childhood. I discovered that although I ranged between skinny and chubby, I was never fat. Not the kind of fat my father branded me with anyway. No one is that fat. That is a kind of ugly that doesn't exist in another's body and certainly not in the mind of a small child. That is the mind of a cruel man who enjoyed the sadist projections of demeaning, devaluing and belittling a flower before it bloomed. In doing so he hoped it would struggle to grow, even if it found a nourished environment. That early conditioning was one of many attempts of keeping me, us, owned. One might look free but if their mind is enslaved there is nowhere they can ever feel free. To be free begins in the mind.

Keily was obsessed with every kind of animal and lost herself in the loving, nurturing care of her many pets. She had quail, mice, gerbils, a squirrel, skunks, a duck, a cat and a dog.

Everyone had a name; the skunks were Rachel and Raquel, the mice were Tom, Jerry, Peter, Kevin… too many to mention and the duck was Daffy. She had special cages for all her pets, some were kept inside and some outside. The mice somehow got out of control and exploded to over one hundred. One day my father had enough of all the animals and tipped off by the sudden growth of newborn mice, he took handfuls of the live mice and flushed them down the toilet until the cage was emptied. Keily came home from school to find my father in the middle of drowning her pets, she was utterly devastated. It didn't stop there. My father cooked the quail, sold the duck to a family who ate it and released the squirrel and skunks. All her friends were killed. When my father had enough, you knew it.

When I was still at home during those pre-kindergarten years, I remember my mother putting me on her bed to nap every afternoon around twelve. I always had this sick feeling and felt tricked by her every time, yet each day I'd seemingly forget until it was nap time once more. I hated falling asleep because it felt like a weakness she kept taking advantage of. I would cry, asking her if she was going to leave me alone again. I would beg her not to do it and ask her why she did it. I was scared and didn't like being alone. She would hush me, telling me that she was right there and would be there while I slept. I believed her every time, but every afternoon after putting me down to nap, my mother went out. Where she went I will never know but she was gone for hours. A silent house is very scary and disorientating to a small child. Perhaps my earlier days of being taken by another woman into her home expounded on that deeper feeling of panic. I just didn't know where my mother was and if she was ever coming back. She did this repeatedly, thus creating distrust for sleeping well into my adult life. It was the beginning of her untruths, likely because she was trying to find a life between the windows of time my father was away, where she could regain a part of herself. It was also the continuation of the conflicting emotions of loving a mother who was protective and adoring but also vulnerable, fearful, a wounded child that was still being beaten and abused. I therefore unconsciously took on the role of becoming her mother, which was problematic as I was only four.

My father told this humorous story many times throughout my life that occurred at around this time. He was on a business trip in London, England. It was late evening in North Vancouver when my father called home and was shocked when a man picked up the phone instead.

'Hello, how can I help you?' said a man with a deep voice.

'How can you help me? Where the bloody hell is my wife?'

'Hello Phillip, how are you?' answered my mother, nervously.

'How the bloody hell do you think I am? A man just answered the phone at *my* house. It is eleven thirty at night. How the bloody hell do you think I am and who the fuck is that man?'

After a long silence, my mother said, 'He is the painter. I am painting the kitchen to surprise you.'

'Well Heather, I am catching the first available plane out of here and when I get home that fucking kitchen better be painted.'

Sure enough, he arrived in the early morning and that kitchen was fully painted. My father roared with laughter at that story. The idea he intercepted her love affair only to force them to furiously paint all night gave him so much pleasure. We all laughed about it over the years, as the way he told it in his English accent was really funny. And by now, we were all just so desensitised because both our parents constantly normalised their chaos with funny, silly stories. It added a bit more insight into just how complex trying to figure them out was, especially for a child.

Keily and Heidi started hiding behind the couch whenever our father came home because they were scared of him; Heidi even more so as she would often get beatings because she didn't set the right example for the rest of us. The beating I remember the most sounded like wood cracking, at least to the mind of a child. I can still see and hear it in my mind.

Ice cubes hitting the edge of the crystal tumbler, the sound of scotch or vodka being poured, Father's voice is escalating, Mother's voice is muffled, she is distracting herself in the kitchen, the air feels thicker, the tone is darker.

Run.

Father made us all get out of bed and sit in the downstairs living room with Mother as if we were about to watch a play. Heidi was lying across my father's lap, which looked strange as she was almost 6ft by age twelve. My father mumbled something about setting an example and with his large, thick hands, started slapping her so hard across her backside that her mouth opened without any sound. One after the other, so many I lost count, he was in a frenzy of rage. Did you know if you hit someone hard enough, their screams are silent?

Heidi didn't go to school for two weeks. That was the worst beating she ever got. We all tiptoed around the house in complete terror of what would be next and there was a sombre grief at what we all collectively witnessed. A child doesn't know how to process that. My mother cried terribly for days. I wondered why at the time she didn't try to stop him. Why did she just stand there? Why, at least now, didn't she leave? I had learned, however, through my other siblings that intervening didn't stop the abuse, it just added another victim. No doubt my mother's reference point of her own beatings normalised the feeling; no one would come to our rescue and in life, bad things just happened. Therefore, it's best to just focus on the fun bits.

My mother was very good at creating fun. She would line us up at the kitchen table to teach us how to make playdough, Papier-mâché or hand puppets from Styrofoam balls and felt. Ever clever, she would occasionally give us a bowl of raw prawns to shuck or batter to stir. Somehow even that became laughter, play, joy and fun, especially if it was your turn to lick the batter off the spoon. I remember sitting on the shag carpet next to the mustard fabric chair in the living room, watching the record hypnotically turn as a man's deep voice narrated the story of Red Riding Hood, The Three Little Pigs and Goldilocks. Each character was dramatically spoken, my heart pounding as my imagination brought them to life. I knew even then that I wanted a house built of bricks, not straw or sticks. As I got older, I recognised that house as being metaphorical for my life and so my goal was always to build one big enough and strong enough that it couldn't be blown down by a big bad wolf.

One of my favourite moments was dancing side by side with Heidi, Keily and my mother to the record she played whenever Dad was at work, *These Boots Are Made for Walkin'*. She got us girls to wear boots, stand tall and sing the song loudly as we walked the room with confidence. I am pretty sure our boots were snow boots, however, as that's all we had at the time.

You keep saying you got something for me…

My mother would put the record on and she always seemed to have this intensity, like she was fighting for our lives whilst still trying to hold onto hers. I suspect it was played the day after she and my father had one of their big fights.

Something you call love, but confess
You've been messin' where you shouldn't have been messin'
And now someone else is getting all your best...

I remember she played it often. I was four, five, six when I stood excitedly waiting for my cue; *Are you ready, boots?* Boy, did I walk.

These boots are made for walkin'
And that's just what they'll do
One of these days, these boots are gonna walk all over you.

I felt that walk for my mother, for my sisters, for my brother and for myself. I loved that song and that moment. The moment I saw my mother rise. Her strength gave me hope and I knew I had enough inside myself to keep on walking for me, with them and for them.

I vividly see, feel and remember that song and to this day it ignites strength, pride and a sense of who I am, in every part of my being. It is the song of my identity. I have so many childhood memories that stem from that house.

Walking down the dirt road ten minutes into the belly of the forest was an old wooden bridge arching over a rapid, winding river. The grade of the river changed depending on the time of year as when the snow melted off the mountain's top and the gushing sounds of water roared thunderously, bringing that forest to life. I loved the sound of that raging river. It was always frightening walking down that dirt road but somehow exhilarating. I picked berries with my mother off the blackberry bushes in summer and often accompanied the paper boy to the hut halfway down the road. I would walk all by myself across that bridge to the shop where I could buy lollies; twenty-five cents got you a box of pink elephant popcorn, five black cats, two jawbreakers or two double bubble gums. It was worth the trip. I went to that shop every week. Sometimes I got pocket money from my father but most of the time Chris and I would find tossed-out empty soda pop bottles and cash them in at the store for five cents each. On the good days, we got enough to buy an Archie comic too. I mostly went to the shop with Chris, he was my protector, at least he told me that then.

He and I were always together, Irish twins Mother called us, as we were closest in age. If he wasn't around, I walked to the shops myself. Not unusual as by now I was in grade one, and like the others, I walked to school by myself. School was much further than the shop. I walked downhill fifteen minutes, stopped and visited a woman who invited me into her home most mornings, of whom I still have no idea who she was. She simply offered me a lolly, so I went in. They were the Halloween taffy wrapped in black and orange paper most people threw out and they tasted stale, but a lolly was a lolly. After another fifteen minutes of walking, I would take a shortcut through a park that led to the back side of my school. Knowing my parents' lack of boundaries by this time one might add this to the list. To be fair, all the kids I knew did the same. We just had enormous freedoms and were taught all adults were to be respected and trusted.

Chris and I were walking home from school one day; it was the first time we had walked home together in six months as Chris had been away from school after he almost died. It started with what my mother thought was the flu, confirmed by the doctors she kept taking him to, but it was his appendix and it eventually burst. Chris was rushed to hospital with a very high fever and a very severe, life threatening bacterial septic infection. After surgery Chris had a train track scar, a port to drain the liquids of pus and infection and his belly button was pulled completely over to one side. Mother drained and cleaned that port several times a day. I remember how frail, pale and sickly Chris was during that time. He would do his school assignments at home, but he seemed so sad and in a lot of pain most days. So, on that first day back when we were walking home from school, two boys stopped us. They were calling Chris gay, pushing him and telling him he was so weak and pale. I was shouting at them to leave him alone, he just got out of hospital.

I remember shouting to a woman doing her gardening outside on her front lawn, requesting her to help. She acted like she couldn't hear me. Chris said nothing. He just grimaced in agony as he took the punches, mostly to his stomach. He just froze and took the hits. When we walked home, he was crying. I was shaking and telling him we must tell Mother and Father, he insisted we didn't. I kept asking why but he said Father would be angry and it would just make things worse. I never told them. It was a horrible day seeing my beautiful, protective brother I loved so much crying. I knew even then that was another moment that greatly affected him. Being called gay, being told he was stupid and weak, it all just echoed his father's abuse. That's the strange thing about a child of abuse, it's almost as if others can sense your vulnerability. It's like somehow, they could smell our awkwardness, our hesitation or how we so easily looked down, looked away, froze and just didn't react and they were on the hunt.

It seemed we always got in trouble when we told our father about bad things that happened to us. It was as if somehow we were annoying him. Like the time Keily accidently rode her bike off the cliff in the backyard. It was a brand-new bike and Keily only just learned how to ride it, although she still wobbled when she tried. Unfortunately, this one day she wobbled right off the cliff. Her screams were blood curdling as her skin ripped along the massive blackberry bushes along the way. As much as they scratched her up bad, those bushes no doubt saved her life.

Father was furious. I had no idea why. Maybe he was embarrassed the neighbours would think he was a bad parent? Maybe he was annoyed, as he was reading his newspaper? Maybe he wasn't really annoyed, but the confusion of responding in these contradictory ways created terrible internal conflicts in a developing child's mind? It's rather clever to make someone so malleable to your training that you apologise when you get hurt. That depth of ownership could surely be manipulated in the future. Keily never rode that bike again.

Father seemed to be making more money working at the insurance company and this was highlighted when he drove up in a Cadillac. It caused quite a stir in the neighbourhood, both for its flash and size. It had an eight-track music player in it too.

Dad gathered us all up one weekend, loaded up the car and drove us from North Vancouver all the way down across the border to Seattle in America. We drove through California, Arizona and all the way across the border into Mexico. We were off on another holiday. Father did everything big.

It's the conflicting contradictions but they made us all feel better and we wanted and needed to feel better in the same way you need to swim to the surface for air. So, despite the hidden shame, fears and abuse, we were on holiday, we had a big house, a really flash car and, just for now, this moment in time, a window of opportunity. It was the calm in the eye of the storm, where you could choose to just focus on the moment. I always seized my moments; I savoured them and kept them safe. These moments collectively could save our lives. In this moment,we were all just happily riding in our father's Cadillac, singing to the Partridge Family tape, feeling normal, almost like a real family. Father was doing better. He was probably just so worried about money, looking after his family and his wife. He was a good man, at least that's what he always told us. He spoilt us with travel, fancy cars and amazing holidays, visiting candle making factories, the aquarium, the zoo, a bullfight, a straw market and all sorts of experiences. We were lucky children. Until he started.

Ice cubes hitting the edge of the crystal tumbler, the sound of scotch or vodka being poured, Father's voice is escalating, Mother's voice is muffled, she is distracting herself in the kitchen, the air feels thicker, the tone is darker.

Run.

Whatever child was closest to him was served with a barrage of soul-destroying verbal annihilations. Father would get so close, it broke the protective barrier of energy that made us feel we could bear it. Like bolts of electrical charges, fire burning up your back, it would physically overwhelm you. How do you get away, knowing you have nowhere to go? To run would only incur more abuse or worse, leave you responsible for passing it on to another. We all took hits. Unless we had enough time to read his tone or micro expressions and request permission to leave the room to go to bed, however early. On the good days, we sensed the need to hide before it even began, like smelling the air before rain.

Heidi and Keily would often hide somewhere together and Chris would find a way to hide me. He was always protecting me. I was the youngest, his little sister. If we were out at a restaurant, the waiter would be abused. At the hotel, the concierge would be verbally shredded, otherwise, my mother got pushed. We all carried that burden, knowing as we tried to save ourselves, we would leave our mother to endure it again and again and again. I loved her so much, it was excruciating. Pushed into the corner of a desk, smashed onto concrete or tiled floors, bashed against hardwood or metal doors, either way, he pushed her, yet always said she fell. I would run out to try to save her, she was always bleeding, mostly on the back of her head, it filled the air with the scent of copper, like wet pennies. Sometimes though, the blood would run down the front of her face and into her mouth, turning her teeth red.

Shaking, she would tell me it was nothing, she was fine, but she would beg me to run or hide in my room. Most times Chris would run out after me. He would stand in front of me, ready to take the hits, trying to shield me, yelling at my father to stop hitting our mum. I would be saved the direct brunt of some of the hits of my father's verbal rages but I could still see, feel and hear my brother's fear, his heart pounding, his voice cracking.

Sometimes, however, Father would hit the back of my head, but he mostly hit Heidi's, my mother's and sometimes Chris' head, either way, it was always the head.

Being hit on the head is demoralising. He would use his fist like a club, but somehow in the moment it didn't hurt, it just made you angry. Like rugby players before a game, it incites fury. Father always added verbal abuse, sprayed like a machine gun at whoever was in the firing line. It was a cocktail forced down our souls, a ticking timebomb implanted for later in life. Once he started, its power was in the delivery, the speed, the tone and always in the form of a question:

'Do you know how stupid you are?'

'Do you know what a fucking prick you are?'

'Do you know what an asshole you are?'

'You know you're an asshole, don't you?'

'Do you? Do you know you're an asshole?'

'Asshole, asshole, asshole, fucking asshole.'

If it wasn't Christopher that time, it was Heidi, Keily or me. Same words just insert a different child. As time went on, he personalised it a little more. Heidi was a fucking slut, Keily was a fucking idiot, Chris was a fucking asshole and I was fucking fat. It's a clever technique for maximum effect as it makes one repeat it in their mind, sinking even deeper.

Father's rages were increasing. There was a permanent hole in the wall leading up the staircase. I think Father punched it just before getting to the top of the stairs to let us all know his tone was not one to be messed with that night. Those fights often turned to Mother getting hit, terrible fights and gunfire. Mother would always run into our rooms and tell us to run outside and hide because Dad was blowing up the kitchen again. He always blew up the kitchen. We would all run outside, hiding behind trees or just waiting until Mother would go back in and check on things.

Usually, he was so drunk he would pass out, Mother would tell us to come back in and we would all go back to bed like nothing happened. Father used to act like he didn't remember any of it the next day. We were all just happy to live through it, so we carried on as normal, although I think we all stayed a little quieter. In hindsight, the white house wasn't the worst part of our childhood. I didn't know it then, but I soon realised after we moved to the bigger house in West Vancouver, the mansion on Queens Avenue. As Mother would whisper, things got worse.

Chapter Eight
The Haunted House
Age 6–9

F ather was climbing up the corporate ladder and making a lot of extra money. Not enough to buy the house on Queens Avenue, but he knew he was on his way up, so bought it anyway. Moving from North Vancouver up the mountain into West Vancouver was a massive leap into status and wealth. My father found a Tudor mansion on 2.6 acres, with five bedrooms, five bathrooms, an inground pool and a beautiful garden backed by forest. It had a very long, winding, tree-lined driveway that made a very impressionable entrance. My mother said she nearly had a panic attack when she found out he bought it. She didn't know how on earth they would be able to afford it, let alone how she would clean it.

I remember going to visit the house with Mother and Father on the viewing day. I rode down the banister of the winding staircase and my father caught me at the bottom of the last step, we had a big chuckle. He had never done anything like that before. I expected him to throw me up against the wall for misbehaving. He was on a high and I assumed it was because we would all live happily ever after now. I was almost six and a half and I really, really wished for my happily ever after family. I was wrong of course. It was more likely he was excited to finally be on his way to realising his quest in becoming really, really rich and this house was a big part of building his empire.

Father worked hard and quickly climbed the ladder of success. He would wake up at five in the morning and return home around midnight. Behind his success was my ever beautiful, well dressed, creative mother who prepared the most incredible grazing buffets in a flash. Father would call from the office at a quarter to midnight and say, 'Heather, I'm bringing five very important businessmen home in twenty minutes.' Mother would leap out of bed, dress beautifully, choose from one of her many hair pieces she kept on Styrofoam heads, spray perfume, dab her red lipstick and then sprint to the kitchen where she kept all sorts of frozen pre-cooked goodies on the ready. In minutes she would create a spread of hot and cold platters. Cheeses, olives, pickled onions, home-made relishes, crackers, hot mini quiches, sausage rolls, an assortment of cold meats, a skilfully carved radish shaped like a rose and always a bucket of ice for the drinks. Then the men would all arrive in their various luxury cars. I would look out my bedroom window, awakened by the noise of drunken voices and headlights. The men always looked so important, drunk, but important. Ties now undone, beautiful suits with striped shirts, cufflinks and fine leather shoes, they looked like my father. Father had clearly entertained the men in his office. They all stumbled toward the front door, their banter and bursts of laughter was more like fraternity boys than business colleagues.

Father had a fine office; it was more like an apartment. It was on the top floor of a high rise building in downtown Vancouver. Large windows, a couch that converted into a Queen Size bed, no doubt used for more than just sleeping, a very large desk with a large leather chair for him, a small chair for his employee, a fully stocked bar and a globe that was an ice bucket once you lifted it open. Father had explained to me once that he kept a smaller chair in front of his desk so he could intimidate the employee or person interviewed. He thought it made him look bigger and more important.

The men would change but the scenario was always the same. Mother was always ready and hosted the perfect parties for these gentlemen. Sometimes I got woken up and brought downstairs to meet these men. Many of them brought gifts for me.

The man who owned Budweiser beer at the time brought me a massive collection of Clydesdale horse stickers, as that was the logo of his brand and he had heard all about my sticker collection. I'm not sure why but I loved stickers. I held an emotional connection to each image and stuck them on our fridge door one by one until there wasn't any space left. I had a story and meaning for each and every one. Another gentleman was from the UK and a little bit chubby. He brought me an entire plastic bathtub of lollies. I was always so to receive these gifts from these men. It made me feel special.

Sometimes, when a deal was signed on the spot, I'd be awakened to come downstairs and play a few songs on the piano. 'Für Elise' and 'In the Mood' were the only two I knew off by heart. Mum would pump the paddles for the player piano to play one of the hundreds of rolls we had while we all laughed, sang, smoked and drank. I always remember how much that smoke clouded up the room, but I loved being there. These were incredibly exciting moments. A man was only as successful as his family in those days. We were all well dressed, well mannered, well spoken, charming and most of all, well trained. Father made sure of that and therefore became very successful.

Dad signed so many deals that not only did he quickly pay the house off, but he also bought a boat; a forty-foot sailboat with a forward cabin and a kitchen gully lounge area that converted into a double bed and two singles for the children. It was crowded but it was one of my favourite boats we ever owned. Dad would study the maps and Mum would tether the boat when we docked or man the anchor while we just dangled our legs between the guardrails on the bow of the boat. I loved the feeling of freedom sailing gave, salt spray in my hair and on my skin, sun shining down, my toes dipping into the ocean whenever we hit a wave, it was freedom. We would sail all around the many inlets and islands off British Columbia.

We sailed most weekends and certainly most school holidays, but only in spring, summer and fall. We would spend a few nights anchored off some wild part of the coast. The first time I remember well. We were all lined up at the edge of the bow, dressed in our orange puffy life vests and Father was holding up a quarter—twenty-five cents. All I remember him saying was, 'First one in…' Splash, I jumped in. My siblings were all still hesitating, thinking about what to do, as the water in Canada is a very dark, black-green with minimal visibility. But twenty-five cents is one box of pink elephant popcorn, four black cats, two jaw breakers and two double bubbles. I jumped in.

I loved the water and in fact, I was nicknamed the water baby by my parents at this time. I was training in backstroke and diving at the Hollyburn Country Club, a short drive from our house. The instructor asked my parents for permission to train me as he thought I was a contender for the Olympics in backstroke. They said no. Father explained, 'I don't want my children being good at one thing only. I want my children good at many things.' It all sounded fair at the time, but I later learned the real reason he said no was he couldn't be fucked taking me to practice every day.

I loved the feeling of swimming underwater. It was another world and that sensory deprivation allowed me to feel cocooned, safe and free; it was a beautiful world I could escape to. I would practise holding my breath whenever I was in our pool. I would exhale and push myself down using the metal ladder for leverage—Chris taught me how to do that. He was always interested in learning about scuba diving and had read that was a technique used. I got so good at it I could sit at the bottom of the twelve-foot-deep end for a long, long time. I remember my mother looking frantic as I viewed her from under the water, her mouth moving wildly and her hands waving all over the place, causing me to quickly rise to the surface. She was distressed, yelling, 'I thought you were dead. What on earth are you doing? You scared me to death.'

'Sorry Mum, I was just practising my diving breath.' I did it so many times after that, but she never worried about it again.

Chris would help me practise sometimes, timing me and encouraging me to go past one minute. One time, I was coming back to the surface for air when he grabbed my head with one hand, pressed firmly on my shoulder with the other and held me under longer. At first I thought he was just trying to help me by pushing me past my limits. When I started to kick and flay my arms, he held me down even harder. I panicked, I had no more air left, I was trying to pry his hands off me and then he finally let go.

When I got to the surface, I looked at him, visibly upset and very scared, it didn't feel right. He just smirked. It was mean, but he was my brother and kids can do mean things I thought, and then I forgot all about it.

Chris and I did everything together at this time. We built forts out in the woods, hiked all through the back trails and we would play together for hours. Chris would play the death march on the piano, my cue to start running. Most of the time nothing really happened when he found me but occasionally he would roughhouse me with a slap to the head or throw me to the ground and then I would start crying. 'Fifty cents if you stop crying and don't tell Mum or Dad.' It seemed like a fair deal as Mother or Father wouldn't do anything about it anyway.

Chris and I went every week to Mr Findlader's house for singing and piano lessons. Chris was a child prodigy who could hear a song on the radio then play it on the piano without reading any music. I was still practising Chopsticks. Chris also had a beautiful singing voice. I could sing too but I was so riddled with social insecurities that singing in front of anyone was painful, even if Mr. Findlader was eighty. So, after a few lessons, I figured out a way to avoid classes. Mother would drop me off at Mr. Findlader's house, I would walk up to his door and touch it with my pinkie finger as lightly as I could. Expectantly, he didn't hear my knock, so I'd pick daisies and wait for Mother to pick me up instead. I managed to get away with this for a few sessions until Mr. Findlader called my mother. Next lesson I was standing outside his door, I pinkie touched when suddenly it flew open and Mr Findlader said with a wide grin of satisfaction, 'Deirdre, come on in.' I realised I got caught so I didn't try it again. I never retained my piano lessons from Mr. Findlader, but I always remembered the two songs my mother taught me, 'Für Elise' and 'In the Mood'. I can still play them to this day.

Chris was so talented in so many ways. He was achieving the highest academic grades in all subjects, was excelling in several sports, was learning several languages and played several instruments. He was also becoming very strong and handsome. Many of my friends at school had crushes on him.

Keily was riding horses in the country. Father even bought her a thoroughbred racehorse she named Dupey. The first day Keily rode Dupey he kicked her off and as she was falling her foot got caught in the lead. Dupey spooked and galloped around the stadium, dragging Keily on the hay-lined floor. Hay burns at that speed and Keily's legs were badly injured. She still wanted Dupey and once healed, rode him as often as she could. She loved that horse so much, as she did all animals. Animals were Keily's family and escape. Mother spent so many days a week driving her ninety-minute drive back and forth. She would complain she had other children, but Father insisted she focused more on Keily. Chris and Keily really were highlighted at this time. Father was homing in on them. I didn't understand why, but he told me at this time that I didn't need him. He said I could take care of myself. I used to run to my mother crying, asking her what Father meant, why he would say I didn't need him. She would say, 'I know you are very sensitive and loving darling, but Father respects you and he just means he thinks you're tough, like him.'

Father started saying that to me when I was seven, then eight, then nine, then ten. What child doesn't need their parents? It didn't make sense to me. It wasn't until years later I understood what it meant. I didn't need him meant he couldn't do anything with me, which meant he couldn't groom me sexually or emotionally. Therefore, I had no real value to him. I just got in the way of his focus on grooming the others. He knew I saw him and therefore, my value diminished.

I was age seven, lying by the pool on a white lounge chair when Father walked over wearing short shorts and no shirt. He sat right next to me, less than an inch away. He had a very large erect penis sticking out of his shorts. I saw it in the peripheral of my vision. I froze and pretended not to notice, expecting him to feel embarrassed and quickly put it away. I wanted to respect he would want that dignity. My assumptions were wrong. Yet again, Father's response to things was always the flip side of what you'd expect. There was never any congruency to his behaviours, I always found that odd. I did learn over time, however, there was always consistency.

Regardless of how many times I expected normalcy, dignity, a father who loved me and wanted to care for me, he shocked me by doing the opposite. That's the problem with psychopathy, behind the mask of a father, a child will always see the good man who truly doesn't want to be bad. The man that is so victimised by his own demons, remorse and shame; and we were all trained not to burden him with that. We were encoded through years of conditioning to help absolve him of those things. After all, he didn't like being that way, at least that's what he always told us. It was a contradiction in that moment where he just laid there, his erect penis sunning under the summer sky, supported by his thick thigh, no less than an inch away from my bare legs, dripping wet from my morning swim, seven years old, in my light blue bathing suit.

It was a bizarre moment in time, like everything just slowed down and something in the rhythm of life seemed off. I felt his deliberateness as he seemed to conduct every move in a way that I thought looked on purpose, strategic even. His eyes darted back and forth and he was observing me in the same way I noticed he played chess. He laid there for what seemed like forever, then smiling said, 'Oh, squeeze me, ha, ha, why didn't you say anything, hmmm?'

Still not even motioning to put it away, he said, 'Don't you see it? Are you too embarrassed to look at it?'

I was embarrassed but I also felt angry, it was weird. It felt wrong and I knew he was trying to trick me. I knew he was trying to make me look and I was wondering why. What was beyond that? I had never seen a penis before, but I could feel this was very unsafe. I stood up without looking and walked off. I knew this time I wouldn't get in trouble because what could he say? It was supposed to be an accident after all. I remember thinking if I spilt a glass of water on the floor, would we all stand there and discuss what it looked like? Of course not, you'd just wipe it up. I learned that day that the air changes for those who feel and the body's synchronised natural movements can be observed, like dance or music, they must have a rhythm. Just like playing the piano, there were too many sharp notes that day. I said nothing because I had nothing to say.

I learned my best reaction was indifference. If I acted like I didn't notice, didn't care, didn't react and just walked away, I would be spared. I learned the art of deflection. That lesson saved me psychologically, emotionally, physically and spiritually on so many other occasions in my life. I love that little girl. I am so incredibly proud she listened to what she saw and felt. I am so grateful for dance, piano, singing, swimming and all the creative, rhythmic lessons that taught me to feel, express, respond not react and feel my way through life.

I had been taking dancing lessons since I was three. First ballet, which I didn't like because it was too strict and my old spinster teacher used to constantly hit me on the back with her cane. She said it was because my back was never straight enough. Turned out, years later at age forty, I discovered I had scoliosis from the base of my head all the way to the bottom of my spine. I discovered it by accident after years of back pain and an X-ray to figure out what was causing it. The doctor and myotherapist both confirmed that someone dropped me from a height as a newborn. Likely Father, multi-tasking with a scotch in his hand, figuring I was alive he didn't tell anyone.

The first signs of my body reacting to my childhood environment began at this time. I had speech therapy lessons for two years as my brain was doing unusual things with words. Nosebleed became bleed nose, doorbell became bell door. Instead of construction worker, I said destruction worker as my mind created its own word, based on what the workmen were literally doing. The therapist helped me to slow my speech, pause, articulate and consider words, their meaning and the power of tonality. She gave me strength and power to my voice. So much so, my report card said: 'Deirdre is a lovely girl, but she talks too much.' Talking was my superpower. I wanted to speak my way out of the secrets and chaos. I wanted to feel safe. The older I got, the more I knew how unsafe we all were, the more I talked. I have learned over the course of my life, those who try to silence you are the ones who unconsciously tell you to be wary of them. It's information about who they are. Besides, I turned my talking too much into my career.

SECRET #5

Dad groomed me but failed. There were conversations and email exchanges Keily and I had over our adult life that suggest he groomed her too and perhaps that developed into more as she got older. The last time I asked Keily about it she said, 'Deirdre, you should know better as a therapist to ask someone who has been sexually abused if she has been sexually abused.' That is the closest we ever got to it.

I suppose my comfort with talking is why I felt safe to emotionally let the floodgates open that day in grade two when I was walking to Patience's house. She was named that because her parents, being much older, had used a lot of patience trying to get pregnant for years. Patience was a wonderful friend to me, quirky and arty, I loved that about her. She lived in a small arched frame home which didn't seem like much back then, but I suspect would be worth a fortune now as it was a stone's throw from the beach.

I used to sleep over at Patience's house sometimes. We would make finger crochet chokers to wear around our necks and eat mac and cheese every time I stayed over. Her parents had made a deal with her to choose one meal she could eat every night for the next year and the money saved would be used for a Disneyland vacation. She chose mac and cheese, which I loved anyway. I was on my way to Patience's house that day when I met the man in the white suit. I was walking down the steep mountainous streets from my house toward my school, as Patience lived a further ten-minute walk toward the water. I thought I'd take a shortcut by walking down the steps into the school's playground, cut across the football field and shave off another ten minutes. I noticed a white station wagon with white leather seats, a white covered steering wheel and white hubcaps, it stood out to me because it seemed weird.

As I walked down the steps and just before I stepped onto the concrete playground, a man dressed in a full white suit with white hair stared at me longer than he should. I felt startled by the intensity of his eyes and how odd he looked. Tall and lean, he started walking faster toward me. I froze for what was probably seconds but felt like minutes. I paused then turned around slowly as if to look like I simply changed my mind. Once back on the sidewalk, I furiously looked for anything to help me get out of this situation, after all I was already primed to do that. Pause, think, act slowly, scan, observe and assess, action. The goal was always survival and escape and the quickest way to do that is to minimise your reaction, that way it's harder to read you. A small empty tin can of apple juice, a common school lunch box staple, now discarded, became my lifeline. I started kicking it then skipping quickly down the street as if I was just a typical unaware little girl playing innocently. But I was very aware I was in danger and I was strategising how to get to safety. I kicked the can then skipped a few metres, kicked then skipped. It allowed me to cover ground much faster. Had I just decided to run, no doubt he would have easily caught me, his legs were taller than I was. I noticed his car in my peripheral vision and the white station wagon pulled up to me on my right side. I kicked the can to move closer to the grass on the left. His window was rolled down and he was coasting very slowly beside me.

'Do you know where (inaudible) street is, hee, hee?'

'No, sorry no idea,' I said.

'Get in the car, I will take you wherever you're going, hee, hee.'

He had the weirdest, creepiest giggle, it was slow, deep and he sounded deviant.

'My friend's house is right there!'

I pointed to a random house a few metres away, convincingly I thought, as he immediately drove off. But then another car drove up beside me, window down, with a woman driving and a man seated on the passenger side.

'Excuse me, where are you going?' the man asked. My heart was pounding, I couldn't understand what was happening. He must have seen my distress as he said, 'We are undercover police officers. That man in the white station wagon has been following you since you left the school grounds. We are watching him as he is a very dangerous man. You must get to where you are going safely. We can take you there.'

I wasn't going to get into his car, so I said no but agreed to tell my friend's parents and ask them to take me to the police station. I was so relieved once I got to Patience's house. I remember talking a mile a minute, blurting everything out to Patience while trying to catch my breath. It all just flooded out once I was inside her home. Her father heard me telling the story and reacted immediately with so much concern. I had never experienced that and it caught me off guard. Oh, this must be really serious I thought as her father loaded us into the car. He was speaking softly to me and asking me what the police officers looked like and what colour their car was. He seemed to think they couldn't be too far off. Sure enough, they were filling their car with gas at the station minutes from Patience's house. Her father spoke to the two officers and then came back inside the car.

'It's very serious Deirdre,' he said with great concern. 'I must take you home to your parents and the police will meet you there shortly.'

I was dropped off at home. Patience's father had a quick chat to my parents who both looked so concerned. My father was rubbing me gently on the head, he never did that before so I thought he must really be concerned about me. The police arrived and said the man in white had only recently been placed on bail. He was an accused child sexual predator and everything was in white because he was obsessed with blood.

I couldn't absorb the full weight of what I escaped, but I knew enough to feel horrified about who that man was. My parents spoke with great concern to the police, thanked them profusely then closed the door. I watched the police car drive away, Mother looked at me so worried. Initially I thought she was just worried about the series of events that day and what might have been, but she was also worried about my father's reaction once the police left. My father raged suddenly, 'How dare you embarrass us like that, bringing police to our door. Is this acceptable to you, huh, is it? Do you see the embarrassment you've caused us, what would the neighbours think, huh?' He said a few other angry things but I can't remember them, I think I blocked them out from the shock. Huh? I thought. I embarrassed you? You're mad at me because someone tried to grab me? I went to bed early that night, mittens wrapped her paws around my neck and purred me to sleep. I heard the distant all too familiar sounds.

Ice cubes hitting the edge of the crystal tumbler, the sound of scotch or vodka being poured, Father's voice is escalating, Mother's voice is muffled, she is distracting herself in the kitchen, the air feels thicker, the tone is darker.

Run.

We had several animals at this time. Bunky the Old English sheepdog, Mittens the stray cat we found at the docks where our boat was moored and Puddy, her daughter. We loved our pets and have so many funny, loving memories with them. There was the time when Bunky ate the entire table of food my mother prepared for a party of eighty people. Or the time Puddy the cat returned home from the kennel stoned, as the owner's son got her high. Then, the many times Mittens would hide behind a corner in the dark hallway and leap out at us just to scare us or murder us with her claws, depending on her mood. Our animals meant more to us than most animals as they offered us all the love we were missing and craving. They pacified the heightened fears our bodies were constantly in. I loved my cat Mittens so much, she was my closest, best friend. She would put both front legs around my neck and purr into my ear; we slept like this every night. She made me feel safe.

It really helped after Mother and Father moved me to the room with the attic door. Keily was in that room before me but she didn't want to sleep in there anymore because she said the ghosts kept her up at night. So, they put me in that room. Why they felt I would enjoy that room any better than Keily is beyond me. But sure enough, I would hear voices whispering at night too.

'Deirdre, Deirdre,' they whispered. 'Shhh, she hears us.'

Then, inaudible whispers speaking quickly and abruptly. It scared me so much I could hear my heart beating in my ears. I would wake up every morning and run to the attic door to check if it was still locked. That door had an old fashion key still in the lock and would be opened about an inch. This happened every night and every morning. I would tell my mother and ask her, 'Who's been in the attic, did anyone go in the attic last night?'

She always tried to calm me and assure me the door was locked, but it was always open in the morning.

I tried using every doll and teddy bear I had to create a barrier between me under the covers, then I would cuddle my cat Mittens tightly, but I still heard them. Chris, Keily and Heidi heard the ghosts too, they weren't exactly subtle.

We used to all sit downstairs in the living room, watching TV after our parents went to bed, drinking pots of tea and chatting about everything in our lives. We would stay up late into the early morning hours, philosophising, reading poetry, Chris playing his guitar and just laughing. We would take turns walking through the dark entrance hall, through the pantry into the kitchen to make tea. It was scary as the walls were dark wood, there was an enormous, round, dark oak antique table carved with gothic symbols and the lights were always off. One night Christopher was left alone in the lounge room. I had already gone upstairs to sleep and Keily was in her room reading. Chris said he saw a naked woman under the table. For some reason he assumed it was me or Keily and said, 'What are you doing under there?' The naked woman said, 'Nothing, nothing.' It spooked him and he found it confusing, so he ran upstairs to check if I was there and seeing me sleeping woke me up. 'Deirdre, stop joking, was that you?'

'What? Chris what are you talking about, why did you wake me up?'

'Deirdre, I'm not kidding, were you naked under the table?'

I woke up, clearly in my pyjamas, so he realised it wasn't me. After explaining what was going on briefly, I said, 'Maybe it was Keily?' Just then we heard Keily scream loudly so we went running to her room. Keily slept in the upstairs maid's quarters. It was a tiny room with a back staircase straight to the kitchen and a double window that sat on a side roof that connected to the garage. Keily was pale and visibly frightened. She said a man was crouched on her windowsill, dressed in white and he kept saying, 'I'm so sorry, I'm sorry.' Then we heard the kitchen cupboard slam, one after the after, then the burglar alarm went off. Finally, our parents woke up. I suppose they slept heavily from all their alcohol consumption. Father called the police who found no signs of break-ins. I remember looking out the bedroom window that overlooked the pool. 'There is writing on the pool patio,' I blurted out.

My father went outside to have a look. It looked like writing in water, but he said it didn't make any sense. Mother said the ghost is getting worse. Father looked concerned but he just went back to bed. It wasn't the last time the ghost acted out. We had many nights of inaudible whispers in the hallway upstairs. We all heard them. Having bronzed arms that reached out of the wall holding up amber lights didn't help the mood either. After whispers, we would hear the kitchen cabinets banging and then the toilet in the maid's upstairs bathroom, which was Heidi's then Keily's room, flushed several times. Whispers, bang, bang, bang, bang, flush, flush, flush, flush then the alarm would go off. Sure enough Mother and Father woke up and whether we were downstairs or upstairs in our bedrooms, we would be awake by now. Father would do the rounds and check all the doors and windows and say there was no sign of entry. He knew something wasn't right, but his logical mind couldn't figure it out. Mother always said it was the ghosts, Father didn't believe in them.

The house was very old and dark. The previous owners told my mother they were leaving because the ghosts were causing too many problems. I know as children we all felt something wasn't right in that house. Whether it was the ghosts or not things got worse there for all of us.

In spite of all the scary things we were experiencing, we still had so many trips by this time. The constant contradiction of chaos and travel, good and bad, hot and cold was normal. I remember getting off the plane in Hawaii and the immediate feeling of breathing in warm air and smelling hibiscus. It was the sweetest, most beautiful flower I had ever smelt. I loved the beautiful Hawaiian women who greeted us with flower necklaces, strung together and placed around our necks. That was the trip I remember Mother and Father leaving me in the hotel room a lot at night when they went out drinking. I also remember coughing at the table one day while having lunch and grabbing my father's water, chugging it down only to discover it was vodka; but mostly it was a great holiday.

We were also travelling to The Bahamas during this time. We always stayed on our Grand Bank boat. We had the same style of boat for years, it just kept getting traded in for a bigger one. I loved cruising to all the outer cays. The Bahamas, its people and the crystal-clear water were and are truly paradise. The Bahamas always felt like my real home.

Tahiti was a family holiday that proved to be life-altering for Keily. We flew to Tahiti and took a small boat to Morea Island. We stayed at an all-inclusive Club Med resort where money was in the form of beads we wore around our necks. You could pop one off to buy a drink or food. We each had our own huts on the complex and a golf cart to get around. Heidi and Keily shared a hut, Chris and I shared one and then our parents had their own. Chris loved the golf cart and drove it past the nudist beach every day. They were very liberal at this resort as they also had nude body painting at the bar every happy hour. There was a song that played before every meal to inform us when breakfast, lunch or dinner was ready.

The buffets were elaborate with dolphins or peacocks carved out of ice, an entire roasted pig and octopus in gravy. It was exciting and luxurious, and we all loved our freedom. Heidi was sixteen, Keily was twelve, Chris was ten and I was eight. We loved how raw and primitive Tahiti was in contrast to our own lives. It reminded us that life's luxuries are mostly, if not always, found in nature and food. We all felt very relaxed there and were told we were protected in the resort.

Heidi and Keily met two young Tahitian men. The one who hung around Keily was nineteen and the one who liked Heidi was twenty-one. There is a picture of Heidi and Keily sitting in the resort dining room, the arms of these men wrapped around them smiling. Heidi looks comfortable but Keily has her eyes cast down and looked very shy and uncertain. She had braces then which added to her self-consciousness. We were all at the bar later that night, around nine or nine-thirty. Chris and I were playing ping pong, Mother and Father were drinking with friends they made there, drunkenly oblivious to much else. Heidi walked past and Father said, 'Where's Keily?'

'I don't know,' she said.

What do you mean you don't know? Heidi for fuck's sake, you were supposed to be looking after her.'

'I don't know, she went with her friend.'

'Went with her friend where? Goddamn it, Christ's sake, Heather, Heidi doesn't know where Keily is.'

He started yelling at Chris and I to go find Keily. We had no idea where or how to look but Chris and I got into the golf cart and drove around looking for her around the resort huts. Heidi went to their shared hut to double-check if she was there. Mother and Father were walking around the bar, the pool area and toward the beach yelling her name as they stumbled along. After thirty minutes we all just sat at the bar. Mother and Father ordered more drinks and Father told each one of us how stupid we were. As usual, he did it in his style of fast-hitting questions.

'What do you mean you don't know where she went, Heidi? You don't know because you weren't fucking watching her, were you? For god's sake, Deirdre, don't you get Keily is missing, do you understand what we are dealing with?'

We were all made to feel it was our fault. If anything happened to Keily we caused it, as we were all responsible for the system. We were never individuals but part of the whole. To be an individual would have meant we had a right to our own identity. We were not allowed to be an individual, we were a collective and that system was in chaos again. It was midnight and Keily walked out from behind a tree-lined path. She looked pale and scared. Father started yelling at her, 'Where, the fuck have you been? I have been worried sick. Do you know what you've done?'

Keily apologised, she just kept saying sorry over and over again. We all went back to our huts, except Mother and Father who sat by the bar continuing to drink. No one asked Keily what happened. It was always about how we inconvenienced Father with worry and stress.

Keily told me several years later, when she was around nineteen, that the Tahitian man she met at dinner had told her he had a beautiful shell collection. She wanted to see it so went to his hut innocently. He raped her that night. Keily never told our parents because she knew she would get in trouble and it was too much to bear being told she caused it with her own stupidity. So she swallowed it instead.

SECRET #6

Keily was raped as a twelve-year-old child and only told Heidi and me. That secret significantly changed and altered her. Whatever happened that night broke a part of who she could and should have become. She started acting differently when we got home. First, she would hide in her room, then she started staying out late with her friends, drinking and acting completely out of character. She had tried to bring a bible home a friend's father gave to her, guessing she might need it to support whatever she was going through at home. Clearly, she too wore the signs that things were not right. When Father saw that bible, he immediately ripped it out of her hands and yelled at her for daring to bring that rubbish into his house. He ripped it apart and threw it in the fire. Without support, Keily become more introverted but sought solace in her cartoon drawings. She was incredibly funny and gifted. Her style at that time was closest to Lawson, who drew animal characters in humorous scenarios. Like all of us, the creative arts allowed an outlet when expression was not only not allowed but aggressively attacked.

Things were getting worse. Father was either never home, away on some business trip or out until very late. The times he was home, there was a crystal glass in his left hand, a cigarette or cigar in his right and a blue and tobacco striped robe worn over his clothing as he sat on the brown leather chair embossed with brass studs, teasing us all. It always started with pleasant banter about his trips, funny things that happened, flirtations with my mother and trivia questions to each of us, as he seemed to playfully invite us into a competition of wits and knowledge. We all played along, intuitively knowing it wasn't going to end well but hoping, every time, every single time, it would just be a bonding opportunity. Instead, it was a show and tell of his intellectual mastery and a public embarrassment of our failings. We were each made to stand up next to him and asked a question: 'What is the closest European country to Greenland?' I remember hearing 'Iceland, Iceland, Iceland,' whispered in my head, but I froze. 'You don't know do you Deirdre, bit of a dumb dumb, aren't you? It's Iceland, dumb dumb.' He would laugh at how clever he was and often that kept him in a good mood.

I remember feeling such a mix of emotions of fear and anger, he had me in a lose-lose situation and a win-win for him. Had I openly said the right answer, he would have been angry and the wrath of his rage would have progressed. However, playing dumb and allowing someone to call you dumb when you know the answer is a toxic substance to swallow. Over time the truth about oneself and abilities can become blurred.

There were those other nights, however, when Mother and Father argued loudly. Father accusing my mother of having affairs and my mother always going back to the original affair he had, with Sharon. He would never admit it and she would never let it go. Their fights were often under extreme intoxication and always ended in violence. I would stand in the hallway outside my bedroom with my siblings, Mother would be holding her head, the smell of copper filled my nose as red blood was pouring down her. Sometimes it was the front of her head, sometimes it was the side, sometimes it was the back, but it was always her head. 'She fell head-first into the dresser,' Father would say. Or fell in the bath, the shower, down the stairs, into vases, corners of tables or just on the tiled floor. She was always falling, according to him. Father said it in a way that sounded like he was the victim. 'Look what I have to deal with. Your mother is an alcoholic you know. Do you see what I have to put up with?'

My mother was an alcoholic by this time. She didn't have her first drink until her late thirties but my father was always pushing her to just have a few with him. In time, it became self-prescribed to escape from the life she saw no way out of. First it was just drinks with my father, then liquid lunches at the Hollyburn Country Club or while socialising with friends. The thing is, for those who live a wealthy lifestyle, alcohol becomes a status of opulence, it supports the 'I can do whatever I want, when I want' privilege—a privilege only if you manage your drunkenness. To be drunk is fine, to look drunk is low class. 'Stay civilised then do what you want,' my father said.

Mother couldn't hide her drunkenness, however. I would ring her to pick me up from the movies, dance lessons or a friend's house. I could tell by the third word whether she had had a drink and how many. It was a survival instinct with great accuracy. 'No, Mum, it's OK, I have a ride, you don't need to pick me up,' I would beg. She would insist in her slurred voice and drive right up in full view of my friends, teacher or friend's parents. I felt humiliated and embarrassed by her obvious drunkenness, lipstick on her teeth, mascara running down her face, her frizzy hair; sometimes she was still in her sheer pink satin nightie.

I felt this heavy burden, swirling contradictions, knowing how funny, beautiful and intelligent she was, understanding her abuse and the pain yet feeling this turbulent feeling deep inside of me. I felt guilty for even feeling that way. I didn't know it then but the emotion was anger. I had to learn to wade below those deeper irreconcilable emotions that ran underneath the deflecting ones like shame, guilt and grief. I was grieving the loss of my mother, my childhood and a part of myself.

She would swerve onto the curb or be too far away, the door would open, she'd looked dishevelled, drunk, confused and would slur something inaudible as she waved me in. I hated her in this moment, while at the same time feeling so terribly afraid for myself and for her. I loved her. I knew she was in pain and I hurt so much for her, but it was frightening, embarrassing and it was just too much.

All I wanted to do was play with my friends, go to the movies or dance, I just wanted to dance. Instead, I was in the car with my severely drunk mother. She would stop at green lights and floor it at red lights, cars honking as we narrowly missed a head-on collision. She would drive toward oncoming traffic in the wrong lane, on back roads and busy highways. I would grab the wheel on so many occasions, pulling it toward me, forcing the car out of the way and trying to dodge cars hurtling toward us.

I knew every time I got in that car it could be the time we both died. I was in a game of Russian roulette that was not my choice to play. I didn't want to die; I didn't want her to either. I was on the ride of testing fate, cars flashing their lights, honking, screaming, 'Idiot! Get off the road.' I didn't want this life, I thought. I didn't even like Ferris wheels. I had enough risk, uncertainty, fear and chaos in these car rides that forced me to be a passenger in someone else's life. I took the wheel.

We were only stopped by the police once. The officer looked at the car, a Mercedes, my mother's rings, opals and diamonds, looked in the car at me, looked at my mother and said, 'Ma'am you're on the wrong side of the road, you need to turn around and go home now ma'am.' Mother slurred, said something incoherent, followed the officer to the exit to cross to the correct lane and drove home, albeit assisted with me holding the wheel. I was in complete fear for my life and this officer did nothing, said nothing. This was happening on such a regular basis, it's how I learned to drive a car before formerly taking any lessons.

The drunken car rides lasted well into my late teens and were always terrifying. I experienced them in Mexico, The Bahamas and Canada. Winter in Canada was the worst, however. Steep, mountainous hills led down from our house on Queens toward my elementary school. Mum was drunk early morning this time, I think she just kept going from the night before and she insisted on driving me to school. There was slushy, icy snow that newly fell and as we drove down the steeply inclined road, we started sliding sideways. I had had enough; it was first thing in the morning for God's sake. I opened the door as the car was moving and jumped out. I landed in a snowbank and wasn't injured, at least not physically. I felt horrified seeing my mother slide all the way down that hill, but I instinctually refused to be a part of her decision, at least for that day anyway.

In The Bahamas, Mother would wake me in the middle of the night, drunk, crying, keys in hand, telling me she needed me to help her find my father. He was out again, with one of his mistresses somewhere and she wanted to find him. What she would do if she did and how I was going to deal with being a part of that was my never-ending stress. I would drive her out the gates, down Beach Road toward Cable Beach where there was a string of hotels and bars. My primary relief that she never found him was always precedent to any thought or concern that I was driving underage and unlicensed. My secondary relief was that my father's mistress never saw my mother in that drunken, frail and desperate state. I wanted respect and dignity for her, she deserved at least that.

I developed so much pre-anxiety at this time in my life. Trying to live a normal life while navigating not getting shot in Father's flare-ups at night, listening to my parent's drunken fights, or hearing my mother cry while she is violently forced head-first into objects, seeing her bleed, smelling blood, always being told how stupid we were, the control of not being allowed to speak unless spoken to, upholding the secrets, sustaining the lies of the perfect wealthy family, seeing my sibling verbally or physically attacked, watching Father burn the Christmas tree and all our presents, again, being left alone a lot, grabbing the wheel of the car my drunken mother is so haphazardly driving while pre-empting a lethal crash, while still going to school, playing with friends, smiling and laughing, while living a life of chaos. It was a lot to endure. I didn't tell any of my childhood friends, I just assumed they knew and didn't say anything. How could anyone not know, I thought. Wasn't it obvious just by looking at me? It was in my eyes, in my tone of voice, in my fear of heights, in my love of eating too many cookies, in my excessive talking, in my humour and antics of always making people laugh, I was abused. My siblings were abused. My mother was abused.

One night my father got a call from the police to come
and get his daughter. Keily was found drunk and passed out in
the local high school. She had originally broken in with some
friends and they all drank for fun. However, once she passed
out, it seems they ditched her. It was the janitor who found
Keily and alerted the police. Father was livid. How dare Keily
bring embarrassment and attention to him. I remember the
police being in our front entrance. Father was so nice, having a
bit of banter, a few laughs, kids will be kids, he said. The rest
is a bit of a blur. As soon as the police left, almost immediately,
there was angry shouting and then it started.

*Ice cubes hitting the edge of the crystal tumbler, the sound
of scotch or vodka being poured, Father's voice is escalating,
Mother's voice is muffled, she is distracting herself in the
kitchen, the air feels thicker, the tone is darker.*

Run.

We were all in bed, Mother came in and shouted, 'Run!' I
remember running down the wet grass, it was hard not to fall
and it was cold that night. Father was shooting up the kitchen.
Bang, bang, bang, bang, boom! I could hear him raging, he was
shouting. 'I have washed my hands of the lot of you. All of you,
I'm rid of you. Good riddance!'

I didn't feel scared standing outside anymore, in fact, the
stars were always so mesmerising, especially on a crisp night.
Have you ever noticed the longer you stare at the sky's ominous

beauty, the more it hypnotises you and reminds you there is so much more? I felt safe outside, surrounded by forest; tall, thick pines that fill the air with evergreen, beautiful, perfectly manicured gardens and the light of the moon.

It was a contradiction of perfection and chaos, financial wealth and emotional poverty. Father never came outside but we knew we had to stay there until he passed out. It never took too long. The alcohol would hit him so suddenly, often he fell from a completely upright position. The crack of him falling was shocking but somehow, he never seemed to get injured. The next morning Mother came into my room crying.

Father is sending you and the others to boarding school. I told him you are too young but he says you all have to go.'

'What about Mittens?' I cried. 'What about all of my animals? Why do I have to go? I didn't do anything. I'm only nine years old, Mum. I don't want to go, please, don't let him send me away. Please, Mum?'

We were all in the car one week later, meeting with the various headmasters of the different boarding schools he had arranged to send us to. Heidi went to Shawnigan, Keily and I went to Queen Margaret's and Chris went to Brentwood. Divide and conquer was yet again activated. Why not send all your children to the same school? We likely would have bonded and gained strength in our own system. Collectively we were all smart enough to outwit him, but because Mother kept complaining I was so young, Father had to appease her somewhat and sent me to the same school as Keily. I was almost ten and was starting grade six. I imagine starting school from the premise of being rid of, punished, banished, cast out and abandoned would be an unfair disadvantage for any child. I have no doubt it contributed to my perspective of boarding school being a dreadful place. At the time it was very traumatic and I likened it to foster care for wealthy people. Send your kids away for someone else to look after, gain all the accolades without the shame or stigma and without sacrificing your lifestyle of parties, travel and alcohol. 'Sign me up' would have been my father's answer.

It was years later I realised it was likely to have been a lifesaving option for me, as I was out of the environment that was so dangerously toxic to all of us. I was safe and in a space I could learn to just be me— I could grow.

Chapter Nine
Father killed Mittens
Age 10–15

Q ueen Margaret's was not the most luxurious of boarding schools. We had cubicles with three-quarter walls we could climb over into each other's stalls, not too dissimilar to a horse stall. Instead of a door, we had an old curtain on a rod. There were four wards on two floors with shared toilets and a bathtub. One matron was appointed to each house. I was in Saint Michaels and we wore red ties, my favourite colour. Our house matron was Ms Reeves, I nicknamed her Toad because she had a rather stout look about her. My dormmates and I would climb over the walls at night, or up and down the hallways, but we could always get back into our room before Toad caught us. She wore stockings and her thighs rubbed together, creating a loud scratching sound, our cue to run or yell out 'Toad' to warn the others.

Boarding school was bittersweet. I formed friendships with girls I still love and admire very much to this day. They each imprinted me with love, kindness, humour and many cheeky adventures, after all, we were family while there. Being away from home, however, was very difficult. It felt like a bird thrown out of the nest before its wings were even fully formed. I cried so many nights, worried about my mother, missing her, my bed and my animals; I even missed my father. I loved him despite everything and at boarding school, I remembered the good things, like the marzipan animals he would bring home from the sweet shop near his office. I could never eat mine, I was afraid I'd kill it, like a voodoo doll I suppose, so I kept mine on my bedside table like a pet. I would also remember our holidays and how funny he was, sometimes he had the sharpest, quickest mind and I loved his brilliance. I loved my parents; I loved my family and I always just wanted my family to be together.

Boarding school had a lot of rules: no walking on the grass, no talking in church, eat everything you're served, no getting out of bed at night, no leaving the premises without permission, keep your room spotless, wear the correct uniform, no smoking and no alcohol. Keily got in trouble for smoking. We were all in the auditorium and the headmistress, Ms. Archibald, I called her Ms Itchy Balls, said anyone who confesses to smoking will not be punished as they will be honoured for their honesty. Keily was one of the very few girls who came forward, but she got punished, terribly. Our parents were informed and she had to do all sorts of chores like cleaning the church and picking up litter off the school grounds. I thought that was so unfair to trick her like that, she cried out of humiliation and anger. She had already endured so much in her young life, being cruel to a child of abuse is especially sad. I was proud of her for being so honest though. Regardless of how people act, I knew even then, all we have is our integrity, it's who we are at the core. Even if no one truly sees it, we know and that's all that matters. Keily stood up that day, I loved that about her.

When I think about the antics I got into, they were all quite innocent but more dangerous than we realised. You see, we could never leave the school premises without a signed note of permission and only during specific day hours and never more than once a week. You also needed a very good reason, so we all said we had our periods. After a while, the vice principal or headmistress would catch on to our unlikely body rhythms and it would be ages before we could go out again. The only place we were allowed to go to was the corner store and we were limited to our $1.50 allowance. So, I organised trips out, usually around three in the morning. It didn't take too long for me to develop very close friendships, learn the ropes and become the leader of the group we called the fantastic four.

On my signal, we would all prepare for the big night. The goal was to get out through the back forest, behind the school block, walk up the winding path to the street, cross without any cars seeing you, get to the hospital emergency section and go into the waiting area of the large hospital unnoticed. We needed to get to the vending machine, where we would splurge on bags of chips, chocolate bars and Coke. We mapped this out on hand-drawn sheets of paper, dressed in our riding pants, boots, jackets, scarves and beanies. Remember, I had trained my whole life for these moments of running out into the trees and bushes. I knew how to run and navigate my best course at the same time, all while keeping watch. We were scared of the night guard catching us, a local spotting us in their headlights or a nurse or doctor on call. What we never even considered is the very high rate of black bears, coyotes, cougars, wolves and other Canadian critters that live in high numbers in that area. It just never once dawned on us. In hindsight, we heard noises on several occasions we did our night escapes, we just assumed we were outrunning the guard. There was only one, after all.

We never got caught and managed to have other adventures. There was the time my friend Marleen, a day student, told me her mum would sneak me and another friend out for dinner and get us back before we were due back in our dorms. Marleen's mum was one of those young, cool mums who seemingly acted more like a friend than a mother. She made us a beautiful Irish beef stew that night loaded with veggies and dumplings and, unbeknownst to us, magic mushrooms. We ate until we were bursting and then got dropped off at the gates as promised. Once we started running back to our dorm, we both got hit with hallucinations at the same time. We didn't know if it was real or not, but a ghost was walking out from the stables, directly toward us and it was trying to call out our names. The ghost looked exactly like Marleen's brother but was shaped in a faded silhouette of fog. We both ran so fast to our dorms and hid under our covers; our hearts were pounding out of our chests.

The next day we received news from Marleen that her brother died in a car crash that night. He was speeding and crashed into a cement wall. We never snuck out again after that.

Keily and I would travel home by seaplane or ferry for occasional weekends. Mostly, however, I travelled by myself as she was in a different grade and had her horse at the stables to care for. I loved travelling on small seaplanes. The pilot would pick me up on a lake in Duncan, close to my school, and fly high above the clouds. I don't remember ever having any other passengers as the plane was very small. I would sit by the small window and watch as we lifted high into the sky; Canada is so magnificent in aerial view. The dense forest is offset by dark green water, rocky shores and most often a grey, misty sky.

Sometimes that plane would bounce so much it was as if it was falling off the clouds, bouncing from one to another. I never felt scared as I always trusted my parents wouldn't allow me to fly if there was any risk. I learned years later, Air West was nicknamed Scare West, as it crashed so many times. Well done, Mother and Father, I sarcastically thought to myself.

I loved taking the ferry ride across the bay from Nanaimo to Horseshoe Bay. My favourite part was climbing the stairs outside in all kinds of weather, getting windswept so strongly you would have to hold on tight to the guardrails. I always had to wear my formal uniform and sometimes my skirt would blow up like an umbrella. The people sitting inside, looking out the glass window adjacent to the stairs, would look so disgusted upon seeing my green underwear. I'd laughed when that happened because they were in fact bloomers, a second covering we wore over our underwear for exactly these moments. People just take things a little too seriously, I thought.

I also loved the café on the ferry and made sure to have pocket money saved up so I could get something hot to eat and a cup of tea. I would sit by the biggest window and watch the ocean waves, the bigger the better. I loved being out on the open water. I had been boating my entire life, so the ferry felt like the biggest, safest boat I had ever been on. It was just magic.

The best feeling was seeing the shoreline of Horseshoe Bay, knowing I was arriving home and one of those cars lined up near the docks was my mother waiting to pick me up. I loved that feeling, it was my most exciting time because I always had so much hope and excitement that this time will be the best and everything will be amazing.

I'm ten years old, in my school uniform and my cheeks are burnt red from the wind. I'm smiling, giggling now, because I caught a glimpse of my brother who arrived before me. He is standing right at the landing area; he must be so excited to see me. I'm bursting, it feels like it's taking forever. I'm waiting for the ropes to be unhooked and the signals to walk ahead. I sprint towards my brother Chris, I'm so excited when I reach him, I'm breathless, but he looks very, very nervous, serious. 'Deirdre, I don't have time, but I need to tell you something before you get in the car. Dad killed all the animals, he shot them dead, and Mum and Dad are separated, they are getting a divorce.'

My mind starts spinning, I'm looking to the left to find something to focus my eyes on before I fall. I can't hear, the sounds are muffled, my ears feel blocked, my throat is getting tight, my heart is pounding, fire is burning up my back. I want to scream but I have no voice, I want to cry but I have no tears. Where are my animals, I thought, where is Mittens, Puddy and Bunky? Where's Mum?

Chris looked so distressed; I know he was trying to protect me. His arms were wrapped around me as if he sensed he had to help hold me up and help me walk. His voice was heightened, breathless and he was shaking. I don't remember the car ride home. I do remember seeing my mother through the driver's side window, she looked catatonic and drunk. Somehow, we got home. The house was cold and empty, the silence was deafening. Money had no effect on comforting me at that moment. I was completely lost, shattered, shocked, overwhelmed and so alone. A big house, a fancy car, nothing protected me against the deep wounds of chronic, insidious, psychological warfare. I lived in active war.

When Keily found out she immediately said in that detached tone, that only a child of abuse so naturally develops, 'Dad wanted to kill us and Mum, so he killed the animals instead.' She saw it as a good thing.

It made sense to us all to view it that way too. Sometimes all you have in chaos is logic. It cuts through the crazy side, like a hot knife through butter. It protects you from going deeper into the fears of facing the instability, of having a father who could kill us or our mother. That kind of fear is destabilising but logic gives you insights and a sense of control in an out-of-control situation. Logic is the light, the pathway to finding a way to stay safe or a way to get yourself out. The sooner you realise the true danger of any situation you are in, the more likely you will survive. Logic is your defence.

Things got worse. Mother was drinking very heavily and coming into my room long after I had fallen asleep. Dad was travelling a lot and she would wake me up, gently stroking my face, telling me how beautiful I was. Once awake, she would tell me all her problems, like I was her priest in a confessional. It was always about my father and his affairs and how stuck she was, but I should never darn a man's socks because I was stronger than her. These late-night visits were happening almost every night I was home from boarding school. She would sit there, sipping her gin and tonic for an hour or more. I felt her pain, I saw her suffering. The next day when she was sober, I would beg her to stop drinking, she always promised she would.

She did try and could often go three months without drinking. I tried so hard to help her stop drinking and carried it as my own burden. I knew all her hiding spots and would remove the back of the toilet tank where she often hid a bottle or under the couch or in the kitchen pantry. Somehow, I thought if I removed the bottle she would stop, but she just found better hiding places. It became a game I didn't want to play, trying to stay ahead of finding those hiding spots and removing the alcohol to keep her safe while my anxiety increased from shouldering her responsibility, I just didn't know it was hers then. She always started up again and so too did all the behaviours that went with it: the nightly confessionals by my bedside whenever I was home, driving on the wrong side of the road into oncoming traffic or disappearing to liquid lunches at the country club, only to come back with a young lover, one of the sons of her friends, but only when Father was away on business.

Leaving me alone was something she did as far back as I can remember. Maybe it was because I was the youngest, her fourth child, perhaps the leniency became easier. First, she disappeared for an hour or two at nap time in the white house, then in the Queens house she would leave for what was supposed to be a lunch and arrive home after midnight, always ready with an excuse like her car got stuck and this handsome young man helped bring her home.

When I was left alone in the Queens house it was very scary. The house was big, there was so much talk about ghosts and there were always creaking sounds and those inaudible whispers. I would sit under the kitchen table in total fear, frozen for hours. I would wet my pants because walking to the toilet was through dark hallways and I just couldn't move. I'd eventually fall asleep until Mother woke me up after midnight when she got home. It was a common occurrence as she was always going out and I was paralysed, a complete shutdown from layers of cumulative fear. I lay in the trenches.

What seemingly looked like a kitchen table to everyone else was part of my war zone. I was alone almost all the time in the Queens house. Partly because my siblings and I had holidays at different times but as time progressed my siblings were systematically getting kicked out. Heidi was first. It wasn't known then but the age to kick us all out, according to my father's way of thinking, was sixteen. Get them out before they grow their wings, that way, they will never fully fly on their own. A strategist never stops, they just alter the rules so one can never truly figure out their next move.

Heidi was seven years older than me, so she was thrown out just halfway through our first year of boarding school. The headmaster of her school called my father and said, 'Come get your daughter, all she does is keep the seat warm.' It's true, Heidi did live a lot of her life in her imagination and she still does. She channels that into her artwork and made a career out of it. I remember her sitting for hours and hours, drawing trees with a thread not bigger than a piece of hair, dipped in ink. Embedded in the tree trunks were detailed objects, symbols or little creatures, hidden away like those buried places in her subconscious mind. Years previously, my mother took Heidi to be tested for autism as she was always more introverted, deemed socially awkward and when younger was quite angry. As she got older, she rebelled by smoking pot, hitchhiking and dating bikies or bad boys. Nothing too outrageous for the times though.

She had every right to be angry for all the times our father hit and verbally abused her. She was fighting for herself and her right to be more than the oppressed child.

Heidi was home on holiday from boarding school, no doubt the recent statement by her headmaster already fuelled my father's rage toward her. I was in the entrance hall, Mother was standing next to me, Father was also there, we were waiting for Heidi to come down the winding staircase as we had somewhere to go. Heidi was walking very slowly, she always did, still does even now, it's just the way she is but if you're trying to go somewhere it adds tension. She had been out the day before with her friend Wendy, hanging at the beach. Father had seen her hitchhiking; I had heard him talking about it at breakfast and he wasn't happy.

Heidi was halfway down the stairs when my father just charged at her, a raised club fist, he started pounding the side of her head, raging so strongly he was spitting in her face, 'You slut, you fucking stupid, dumb, dumb, slut, get out of MY FUCKING HOUSE. DO YOU HEAR ME? GET OUT OF MY FUCKING, HOUSE!' Heidi was towering over him, she was standing on a step just above, but she was also almost 6ft now, he was only 5ft 10.

Something snapped in Heidi that day, perhaps the feeling of being in a position of looking down at him gave her the strength, as she shouted back, 'DON'T YOU EVER HIT ME AGAIN. YOU CAN NOT, EVER, HIT ME, AGAIN.' Father was dumbfounded and in that moment of his hesitation and shock, she marched out. He didn't get to throw her out, she walked out and he knew it. I was so proud of my sister at that moment, she looked so strong, so powerful.

Up until then, I didn't really know her. Our age difference made us like passing ships in the night and although in pictures I saw the sweet younger Heidi holding me as a baby, the older me got the angry version. To an abused child, anger is a lack of expression, I knew that then and in that moment. Heidi left without taking a thing with her. I imagined she went to Wendy's. With Heidi gone and all of us at boarding school, Father had access to us individually more often, divide and conquer now had different psychological advantages.

We couldn't cross-reference our experiences as easily and being on our own meant we had no backup. The escalation of trying to be the favourite child really began to fester at this time, instigated always by our father. Chris was the prodigal son, getting perfect grades, mastering every sport and being extremely good-looking, so he was taken on trips, given large sums of cash and verbally highlighted as the brilliant one. Keily was given the same extra attention, large sums of money, praised for being extra skinny, sexy and highlighted for her looks. Their status could change in a heartbeat however, for no apparent reason, and then I would step in, highlighted as the logical one, the one who can take care of herself, the only one who seemed to understand. Heidi was the sensitive one, the one who always cried and helped keep things hidden.

Whatever his mood, he would move us around on his chess board, filling us with the false hope that somehow we could now have a healthy relationship, as we were finally being the good child. The idea that I was the logical one developed into being a mediator, confessional or, how I perceived it, hostage. Not only was my mother coming into my room most nights, but Father would also hold me hostage at the dining room table. He would talk incessantly for hours, drinking vodka, swirling his ice cube in his drink and eating crackers and cheese, while intentionally dropping crumbs all over the table and onto the floor.

He liked leaving a mess, a contradiction to his obsessive-compulsive cleaning habits, rather it was to force our mother or one of our maids or house boys to pick it up. It was a message to denounce you and make you bow down. He was equally doing that to me, as I was never offered any food or allowed to leave, not even to use the toilet. To do so would have triggered a tsunami of rage as we had long been trained never to speak unless spoken to whilst at the table. I would sit upright best I could and look at him eating, a crumbling mess. While he talked and talked and I would hold court, no flinching, never let him see you flinch, it's what he wanted, I got good at it. I thought I was being clever to not show my cards but ultimately that's what he wanted, to engage me to play. I was called to his left side, to sit at his table thousands of times, so many, my back has never recovered.

I didn't know it then but while I thought I was a clever girl, I was keeping my true self, all my emotions, thoughts, feelings, anger, fears and cries locked up, tightly hidden, in my back. It became my secret vault; I guarded, shielded it and instead faced his insults and venting about everything and everyone who somehow created a disturbance in his life.

'Did your mother tell you she's an alcoholic, did she?'

'Do you know how much I have spent on you lot for food, boarding school, this house?'

'Did you know I could go to Australia and be rid of all of you?'

'You do realise, all of you children have been a disgrace, intolerable?'

'What do you think about my affairs?'

'Do you blame me, with a mother like yours?'

'You must understand why I should leave with another woman, don't you?'

If I answered, even muttered a word, he would rage, 'Can I get a word in edgewise?' An ironic thing to say after a two- or three-hour monologue, I thought. The psychological threat of gaslighting me with a reinvented version that cast him as the victim, whilst not allowing me to eat, drink water, speak or use the bathroom, sitting on a hard chair in the same position over several hours became unbearably uncomfortable. It's the same technique used to brainwash victims in cults.

Had my siblings been there, no doubt one of them would have left, cried or shouted for him to stop, at least together we had a chance. At least together we would have a witness should something more sinister happen to us.

Chris and I would look forward to spending time together, it was our agreed commitment to have each other's back. We were very close but even more so as we got older, bonded by the shared family secrets and for always standing up for each other. During our holidays in Canada on the boat, we would catch cod fish for Mother to make fish cakes, or swim with the otters. We would also do exactly what we were told not to do, like climbing onto the floating log booms.

There would be hundreds of large tree trunks cut into equal lengths, tied together and floating off the shoreline. I loved the sound they made, a sea chime of soft, wet pine logs, knocking together, according to the rhythm of the waves. It created its own unique, beautiful sound, it was enticing. To walk along them felt like you were on a floating keyboard. The danger, however, was if you fell between the log, you could either drown from being trapped underneath them or get squashed trying to get back up in the seconds the gaps opened.

You can't control the movement of that many logs. A child doesn't really think about those things, however, the rules were guidelines and we just loved being there. I climbed onto those logs many times but this one day I got hypnotised by its charm, slipped and fell in. It was strange because just as easily as I fell into the dark green waters, I seemingly popped back up and pulled myself up onto the log in exactly the rhythmic timing of the opening and closing of the gaps. It's an extraordinary thing one couldn't achieve even if they thought about it.

I think my auto-pilot response of running, leaping into the air and being caught mid-waist by my dance partner in my contemporary dance classes primed me for this moment. It was executed with the exact same movements. Either way, it was only then I realised why my mother was so adamant we didn't walk on those log booms. It was the last time I walked on them ever again. I still miss the smells and sounds of their magical charms.

On our trips to The Bahamas, Chris and I would gather up the conch shells and Mother would make conch chowder or cracked conch. It tastes a bit like a large scallop but better. In those days, you could walk out at low tide for metres, simply picking these massive, flamingo pink shells out with your hands. I remember the time my mother chopped a large pile of conch into tiny bits on her chopping board and it started moving. She roared with laughter as she tried to keep it from walking off. I was somewhat mortified but once they got rolled into fritters, deep fried and dipped in spicy sauce, I sat there eating them with my feet dangling off the side of the boat, watching the fish in the crystal-clear water and I forgot all about it.

The year I was ten was such a powerfully imprinting year for me, it was the time my inner child was anchored. So many life-altering things happened, including the time my father pointed the gun at my forehead and pulled the trigger. Having guns around was a constant part of my childhood so that wasn't the scary part. Pirates or being at risk of intruders were also normal, in part because of the type of wealth we had, but mostly because of the countries my father took us to. However, that night when he pulled the trigger, there was this moment that was probably only a second but I have played it over and over again in my mind, so it feels like forever. In that moment, Father looked controlled but angry, so very angry that I didn't obey his command not to get a glass of water. It's that scene my mind replays, questioning, 'Did he know it was me but shot anyway because he was angry that I disobeyed and got a glass of water? Surely not—or was that it?' The child in me felt worried about how he must have felt so overwhelmed by his fear at that moment and then burdened by his potentially lethal mistake. The therapist in me, however, knows if you were standing in a court of law and had to completely remove all emotions and just state the facts, he saw me yet still pulled the trigger, the answer was clear.

To understand a disordered mind, you must change your filter, removing all emotions, empathy and consciousness to get to the black-and-white thinking. Sometimes it hurts to bend it so sharply. It's a dangerous place for an empathetic mind, as it's a dark place, a sceptical place and one you don't want to stay in for too long. The truth will reveal empty pits, a void, like a concrete bowl, where regardless of how much you hope for more and wish for a better narrative, you discover you can't grow a flower in a concrete bowl. I got lucky that the gun jammed that night.

Chris and I shared Christmas gifts every year, so when we were in The Bahamas one Christmas, we got a large rubber dingy with a big motor. We took that dingy out to reefs kilometres from the shore and skin-dived looking for lobster. We also rode our dingy past Julio Iglesias' house, the Spanish singer, because he loved to hang out at his home naked and always with one or more naked women. We both thought that was wild and often practised water skiing right in front of his home. Chris said it was the best spot to learn how to ski on one ski because there were so many sharks. He said I was less likely to fall if I knew that—he was right. I think he just liked seeing the nude people too.

Chris also got a spear gun that year, so we went out into the ocean trying to find a shark to spear. Chris immediately saw a sand shark and shot it right in its head, but it just bounced right off and it seemed to really be angry as it started circling our boat. It was at that moment I realised it was a silly thing to do, since all we had underneath us was rubber, but we survived, so ended up laughing hysterically over that one.

Father decided to offer the Irish captain of our boat, moored in The Bahamas, extra money to watch Chris and I, while he and Mother went to bars and restaurants or to other people's boats for drinks. We only just met the Irish captain and although he seemed nice enough, it was weird how easily our father would hand us over to others for supervision. He did it on all our holidays and they were always men. There was one man named Tim who watched us while on holiday in Bermuda. He did 'something' to Chris, but he would never say exactly what, just that he had a painful experience with him. It was clear it was traumatic, but he never wanted to talk about it. In The Bahamas, this Irish captain sat up on the top deck and pulled out a massive joint. It wasn't the first time I tried pot, that was in Mexico while on holiday with a school friend, just before I turned thirteen. It was a one-off as I passed out and didn't remember much of it, except that pot wasn't for me. On the boat with Chris and the Captain, I gave it another go and inhaled deeply. I held it in for as long as I could, I think I just did what I had learned to do with my deep-diving breathing, it made sense at the time. Chris nicknamed me hoover and by the third inhalation, I was laughing so hard he could have said anything. Chris went downstairs to the gully to get some chocolate cake for all of us. The captain pulled me closer with his arm around my waist and went to slowly push my head down to rest on his lap but really pushed my head down onto his crotch. As he did that, he told me I was such a little pistol. I had no idea what the hell he meant by that but I immediately stood up and called out to Chris to hurry up and bring the cake. I said nothing because nothing happened, but I knew it could have. The chocolate cake was delicious though. It's amazing how much could go wrong if only things were just slightly different, both good and bad. It's a mix of our own control, awareness, reaction and inaction, but also just circumstance, timing and a little luck.

I was home at the Queens house a few months later, just for the weekend, with my brother Chris. Our parents were away but he managed to get the house key so he could have a party for his birthday. Chris and I had a lot of shared friends, many of whom were also brother and sister. Chris got really wasted that night. I had noticed he was starting to go hard on all substances now, hash brownies, pot and alcohol. It used to scare me how hard he went, as he would turn so pale it was as if he was void of colour, like all the blood was sucked out of his body. I used to think it was a complete disregard for his life as if dying would almost give him the peace he was so desperately seeking. Everyone would laugh at this handsome, athletic, rich-lad behaviour and commend him for his constitution, but I thought his use of substances looked like someone in pain. The violence and chronic abuse of our father weighed so heavily on him; it was a pain he just couldn't offload, so I think it got channelled into substances very early on.

Chris had already downed a few dozen beers but he ripped off a large chunk of hash brownie with his hand and laughed as he chewed it; chocolate all over his teeth, he roared with laughter. We all had a great night up until then, Chris had his guitar out and would sing loudly as he played. He was charming, brilliant, extremely athletic and very handsome, the girls all loved him. But around forty minutes after he downed the hash-laden brownie we heard a blood-curdling scream from the downstairs bathroom. I ran as fast as I could to the back bathroom in the lounge area. The door was locked and several of my friends were asking the girl inside what was wrong. She was saying Chris was trying to force her down and she wanted out, he was pinning her on the ground and she was screaming for him to get off her and let her out. Everyone was telling Chris to let her go, to just open the door. It was only minutes but it was intense and confusing. The door opened, Chris walked out, he looked angry, the girl looked shaken and upset and just ran out.

Whatever was happening caused all of us to leave as we sensed everyone had enough and needed to go home. I stayed at a friend's house, as did Chris, everyone else went home except for one boy who decided to stay in the house by himself as he was too drunk and was just going to sleep it off in Chris' room. We all thought that was brave of him and joked about the ghosts getting him and to be on the lookout for the whispers in the hallway. The house was broken into that night. The boy sleeping in my brother's room remembered someone standing over him but he was so drunk he just went back to sleep. Whoever the burglar was knew the house intimately. My father had a safe hidden in a closet that contained a piece of gold jewellery for each child, collected from every country he ever visited on business, which was a lot. It also had large sums of cash and keys to the Mercedes. All of it was stolen, along with very expensive cameras. The boy went home the next day but when my parents returned, they called the police and the investigation went on from there. It didn't take long to discover who the burglar was, the man living with my sister Heidi at the time. He was known to my whole family, we even had him over for all our holidays, we all loved him. The police wanted to investigate Heidi as it was standard to question her through association.

My mother told me all the details and that the best plan was to send Heidi away to Europe to avoid any of the harsh investigations. They decided it was best to send Keily with her as she was seventeen now and had missed the enforced cut off age of sixteen to be kicked out, so this was the perfect opportunity. Besides, Keily wasn't really doing much of anything at this time. She had tried to get a summer job at a local restaurant but a waiter dropped a bread roll and placed it back on the patron's plate. Mortified she stormed out, declaring to my father she was so traumatised she would never work again. It's a funny story at first glance, but Keily never did work another day in her entire life.

Unbeknownst to us, for many years Keily was financially supported by our father. Eventually, we all had trust funds but Keily was given the motherload of support. Our father pretended to be her employer and would write letters stating he represented her as a published author and guaranteed her generous wages. This allowed Keily to get into any apartment she wanted as she came with incredible references. For years we all struggled to get into any apartment, being underage, working without having any basic skills, not even knowing how to pay a bill, wash dishes or find a job, the plight of a rich child with staff and an abandoned teen of sudden poverty. Keily escaped those burdens and was very generously paid enormous amounts of money, millions over the years. We always wondered what the cost to her was, however, or what our father was paying for. It seemed blazingly overcompensating, even for the man who loved to divide.

Keily and Heidi flew to England and began their modelling careers, or at least that's what my parents said. In truth, they did do a few small modelling jobs, but they were paid to stay away, supplement part of their time with work and keep any family secrets out of the neighbour's reach. I got a letter from Keily to update me on her time in England. She wasn't enjoying it very much. Her first modelling job was for a hair show. She had luscious, wavy, red-blonde hair but they shaved her bald and only paid her one hundred dollars. England was cold and Keily and Heidi weren't making much money. Keily dressed in punk clothing at this time with purple hair, shiny thick white snakeskin boots, silver pants and a leather jacket, she was expressing her state at that time, at least that's how I saw it. She got teased terribly, however, and it would often upset her. They decided to move on to Mykonos,

Greece, at least there it would be more liberal. They stayed a few years, going through boyfriends, dancing, drinking and having a fabulous time.

Back in Canada a few years later, the girls were relieved to be on safe ground. Heidi's previous boyfriend, who burglarised our home on Queens, was still in jail. Heidi and Keily rented an apartment in Vancouver and then slowly made their way down to California. Keily was pursuing a career as a cartoonist, Heidi was studying art at Cal Arts. I didn't hear much from my sisters during that time, but I was so busy going through my own stuff.

I learned later their lives met with challenges and traumas that could only come from being cast out so early with the deeply encoded wounds of our father that subconsciously set them up for danger, especially when it came to partners. When you have lived your formative years with a malignant, sadistic, obsessive-compulsive psychopath, everyone else pales in comparison thus normalising abuse becomes most certain. The problem with being cast out too early, so we all could be malleable to our father's control, meant we equally were all at risk of being malleable to other predators. Abuse is funny that way.

During this time, I was at home alone with my mother in the Queens house during most of my school holidays. The girls were in California and Chris was either at boarding school or accompanying my father on his many business trips to Bermuda or England. An undercover police officer had been placed in the same prison cell as Heidi's ex-boyfriend in Canada. He was asking questions about the house burglary. The ex-boyfriend disclosed he had a bigger plan when he was getting out and that was to kidnap me for ransom. He said my father had millions and I was his youngest daughter and often left home alone, so he guaranteed it was a solid plan. He knew the house well and had a drawn-out map with the plans of how to get in and access me by climbing on the garage roof, as it led to an adjacent roof right under my bedroom window. He had people lined up to help and was bragging about it to this undercover cop. The police called my parents and came out to advise them how to keep me safe.

I had a panic button placed on the wall right next to my pillow, as the head of my bed was right under the window. I hated it like that as I always felt petrified at the thought of someone coming up from behind me and taking me out headfirst; it added to the already terrifying situation I was already living in. I was also given a portable panic button I had to keep on me at all times when in the house. My parents gave me detailed discussions of my risks as if I was a prepared adult myself.

It was so frightening; I think a part of my brain tried to change the narrative. I imagined the ex-boyfriend being really kind, taking me out to eat at a restaurant, my father paying the million-dollar ransom and me just being dropped off at home. Another part of me, however, imagined him pulling me headfirst out of the window at night. I couldn't imagine the first version of my imaginary story after that. The threat of being kidnapped endured for the years I stayed at Queens and continued into my stays in The Bahamas and Mexico, my parents' future homes. The kidnapper changed, however, and it was never as direct and certain as the ex-boyfriend was. In The Bahamas, it was just the threats many wealthy families were aware were possible and in Mexico it was the cartel whose history of kidnapping is world-renowned. It's part of the culture, particularly when you choose to live in lawless countries or where laws can be changed for the right person at the right price. My father loved those countries the most because he could do what he wanted and buy himself out of anything.

Money is power to a psychopath and a lawless country is a fun playground. Father was king of his castle, master of his wife and children and entitled to everyone and everything, unapologetically, without provocation and without culpability. The rules didn't apply to him.

I liked being thirteen. I had grown taller and trimmed down, which enhanced my looks, and people commented and started referring to me as beautiful. It felt nice. I never had fancy clothes, despite our wealth, as Mother always took us to op shops. The first time I went, I was much younger and just remembered thinking I was in a high-end department store as it had an escalator. Mother gave each of us a basket and told us to get whatever we wanted. I loved hunting for the best finds.

Years later, my mother explained she wanted us to be out of the system. Whether she knew the irony of the parallel to the system of abuse our father created, she was referencing the bigger societal system. She wanted us, me, to think beyond what society or anyone else told us about what was of value or what we thought we needed and the importance of individualising. It was her 'fuck you' to the system and since she hardly ever swore, it left a funny and shocking impression on my young mind. Mother had two 'fuck you' messages she dropped deep into my young mind. The second one was what she called, 'fuck you money'. She made sure I always had a secret hidden stash of money on me at all times in case I had to depend on someone to drive me home and they were drunk or just not quite right. It was a slight irony for the years she drove me when drunk, but I graciously noted it for how it was intended. Mother was always doing her best to encode us with the antidote to our father's programming. It worked, as I always keep a secret stash of 'fuck you money' just in case.

I had incredible friends at boarding school and would spend my winters in The Bahamas snorkelling, water skiing, island hopping, fishing and sneaking into discos. Chris and I would sneak out of the bow of the boat as Mother and Father were either on another boat having drinks or at a restaurant drinking. I'd wear his big shirt as a dress and his Calvin Klein cologne and he would have on a polo shirt, tanned shorts and loafers. Both of us had sun-bleached blonde hair and bronze tans, which made our eyes extra blue and our teeth super white; we felt good. We would walk down this sandy pathway out of the marina on Paradise Island that led to the side of a big hotel that had an amazing disco. Michael Jackson, Hot Chocolate and Chic were all played by a DJ called Mr T. I loved dancing and was on that floor for hours. I would feel like everyone was admiring my moves when on cue, I would shake my body down to the floor at the exact moment Michael Jackson sang that verse.

The disco would be filled with croupiers, tourists and a lot of local Bahamians. We snuck out almost every night; our parents didn't have a clue. I loved my brother so much; he was my protector and was always telling me how beautiful I was. He wouldn't let any guy near me, I was just there to dance and no one knew how young I really was, so I was grateful he kept guard of me.

We almost never drank or smoked anything, but this one night, Chris took out a thickly rolled joint. I inhaled deeply, just like the previous few times, and quickly became very lightheaded. Chris smoked the rest, his eyes were small and red and he was clearly very stoned. We smoked it after we had been out dancing, on our way back, walking through the sandy pathway with beachy shrubs. We were almost at the marina when Chris grabbed me by the waist and used his leg behind my knees to push and trip me backwards. I fell on the ground hard; he was lying on top of me, pinning my arms down with his rugby-toned muscular arms. Even through my clothes, I could feel his penis was erect and it was large. I didn't want whatever this was to happen and my mind was racing, trying to figure out what to do. He was acting aggressively and it got very serious all of a sudden. I knew if he did what I thought he was trying to do, there wouldn't be any way out and that could be an even more dangerous situation. So, I started laughing hysterically, as if I was so high myself that I wouldn't remember any of it. I started saying, 'Oh my god, what happened, ha, ha, you fell, oops, I fell, we better hurry, Mum and Dad are going to be back soon. I forgot they said they were coming back earlier, ha, ha, that's hilarious.' I just kept talking and laughing while at the same time trying to roll and loosen his grip. It worked; he had an out and got off me.

He was probably just too high, a young, horny man going through puberty and he just got confused. I kept repeating it in my mind. But I also remembered all the times he told me how much he loved Lord Byron and that Byron had a consensual relationship with his sister. I just wanted to get back to the boat. We stumbled down the sandy path and within minutes were back in the marina.

Our family's boat was moored steps from the path, so we climbed back on board and went to the bow where we both slept.

Single mattresses formed a v shape on either side of the bow with around one foot between the part of the bed where our heads were; it became narrower toward our torso and feet. I went to bed and pretended to pass out. I clearly still didn't feel safe; it was a confusing evening. I lay there with my eyes closed; the only light was from the moonlight coming in through the port hole. Through the crack of my right eye, I could see my brother was trying to see if I was asleep. He was kicking his sheet off while he was looking at me, I suppose to see if I had any reaction. My heart was pounding. I didn't even know if Mother and Father were back on board yet. There in the moonlight was his completely erect penis. He kicked the sheet completely off and was staring to see if I flinched. I didn't. I stayed awake most of the night, but eventually, exhaustion kicked in and he fell asleep.

I knew it wasn't just the pot that caused him to do that, yet I couldn't hold too strongly onto the belief that my brother would ever try to hurt me, so I never spoke of it. He was my beautiful, loving, protective brother, I needed him to be that and in many ways, he was. It was easier to just let it all go, at least at that moment, but it was, still is, part of a collective that paints a story of a darker side to my brother, one that makes me truly grateful for those microseconds in my life that changed the outcome for me. Not everyone gets that rhythm executed so perfectly. Luck, intuition, reaction, inaction, a quick mind, you must read the air before it hits you and even then, it's sometimes just luck.

Back in Canada, I was now going to the same boarding school as my brother. Brentwood was a very different boarding school, prestigious with beautiful grounds, amazing teachers and most importantly, they gave their students freedom. I couldn't believe

Chris was living the life he had there all these years while the rest of us went to archaic, religious schools bent on keeping us locked in with rules that offered no individuality. I was so happy for him, though, he seemed to be thriving and he deserved that. At Brentwood, I did well; I loved field hockey, the choir, the drama club and contemporary/jazz dance. Chris, however, was extremely successful at Brentwood, being captain of the rugby team, captain of the water polo team, head prefect and he got the highest awards in every subject every year he was there.

I, along with the rest of the students, would sit there just hoping one of us would have their name called at an award ceremony, but it was always Christopher Rolfe, highest achievement in level one math, Chris Rolfe, highest achievement in level one, biology. It got tedious after a while, it would have been easier to just give him all ten books or how many there were in one go, but I was always very, very proud of him. He deserved it, I thought. He had so much abuse from our father's constant pressures and alcoholic attacks, calling him an asshole, fucking, stupid asshole.

You might think after a while, one just tunes it out, but you don't; like water torture, each drip of water on the forehead becomes so painful it feels like your brain is going to crack. Over time, it did; that's what abuse trauma is.

My moments with Chris at Brentwood were very bonding and special. He would walk me to the cafeteria or along the water's edge and tell me beautiful things to fill my mind up, an antidote to the horrors our father imprinted. He would mentor me on how to behave with boys, although unbeknownst to me, he had warned anyone who tried to date me he would bash them. It was a warning just in case, as I heard years later he was quite violent at Brentwood and would get in trouble for beating up the new students during their first year.

I didn't mind not dating, I was interested in boys but I wasn't sexually active. I was mostly in survival mode and that takes a lot of your time. I did have many crushes, however, mostly the gorgeous boys in my dance class, most of whom were gay. I excelled in contemporary dance and my teacher contacted my parents, requesting I be sent to a prestigious dance academy in Montreal, Canada. The immediate answer was a firm no. There was absolutely no reason for it, as my father had an enormous amount of money at this time and being away from home clearly wasn't the issue. History, however, is the greatest predictor of the future and my father's patterns were to keep us held back and dependent, even more so for the strong or talented ones. I wasn't just a good dancer, I was an amazing dancer. I would run with speed and fearlessly catapult myself into the air, completely trusting one of the boys to grab me at my waist and hold me mid-flight. It took trust, skill, rhythm, expression and grace.

I never listened to music; I felt it in my body and instantly choreographed every move in my head. To this day, I can never really hear the words, as music is an escape, like diving deeply to the bottom of the pool. I dance, deep down, from within.

Chapter Ten
Assault and Matrimony
Age 15

Held up in luxury, the best boarding schools, prestigious cars, exotic holidays, yachts, fine dining and money, the external accolades reconfirmed my father's threats that he could and would easily cast out anyone who challenged it. He was always reminding us as he drove us around in his convertible Mercedes or, while steering one of his many yachts or while staff served us lunch that these perks were currency, a payment for the most dedicated to look away, remain loyal to the system and hold the secrets, regardless of what they were. Challenging the dysfunctions and abuses in between would deem any of us to be flawed, ungrateful or not deserving. A real threat of abandonment and disownment held over us like a bounty on our heads. I was the last one standing, all my siblings now cast out, one by one, each by the age of sixteen. I knew my time was coming very soon.

You would think once each child moved out, all the problems endured over time would slowly be resolved. We were all roped back in, however, on the financial lifeline Father called a trust fund. 'My children are heirs to a fortune,' Father would say. 'No children of mine should ever work; it's beneath them. Stay beautiful, skinny and intelligent. You are a Rolfe and Rolfe's do not work.'

He encouraged all of us to avoid learning to drive a car or attending university or anything that possibly gave us any kind of independence. Dependence was rewarded, while independence was seen as being ungrateful and rebellious to the system and would cost you tenfold. You would be cut off financially, un-invited to family holidays; kicked out within a day of arriving at the start of a holiday, regardless of how far you flew to see them. I watched my siblings leave, yet all went back to him over and over again, each time getting an even bigger bonk on the head.

The motivation was always acceptance, love, a father and, of course, money or material things. Trauma bonding is a cruel and insidious beast, a pet to the psychopath that is so generously fed.

We would all be gathered on his yacht, at a fancy restaurant or sitting at his long oak dining room table when he would remind us, after a disastrous night or several days of abuse, how incompetent, stupid, insidious, disappointing, failing and miserable children we were. It wasn't always directly said, but it was always clear in the questions he asked and the rage in his eyes.

'Do you know how much this boat cost me?'

'Do you know how much I pay the staff each month to serve you lunch?'

'Do you know what I have to put up with because of your mother?'

'Do you know your mother is a god-damn alcoholic?'

'Do you know how much I have to put up with you lot?'

'Do you know I could just take all of this, everything I own, and go live in Australia?'

'Do you know you would have to take care of your mother, work and live in squalor?'

'Do you want that?'

'Do you think I like being like this?'

'Do you know what assholes you are?'

'Do you know how bloody stupid, stupid, stupid you all are?'

Anger was a common theme in our family. It wasn't just our father, but even the children were showing the signs of marinating in his toxicity for too long. Oppressed and devalued, Mother was drinking very, very heavily and the weight and the consistency of the chronic, escalating abuse was getting hard to bear.

Father was selling the house and his business and moving to The Bahamas. He gave Mother an ultimatum to leave or come with him, but there were conditions. He was about to make more money than he ever could possibly imagine with the sale of his business. It was approximately twenty-eight million dollars, plus the sale of his house, plus his savings which, according to him, put his net worth at around eighty million dollars. He was moving to Lyford Cay in Nassau and his family was not required.

Lyford Cay is a gated community designed for the elite wealthy. Movies stars, famous singers, royalty, famous hotel chain owners, famous liquor brand owners, you had to be interviewed to get in. The house he was buying had a dock right in front of it so he could moor his yacht and there was a marina five minutes down the street. More importantly, however, was mistress beach. It was a small beach off to the side of the marina where many of the local husbands visited their mistresses. Father had three already waiting for him, so Mother was told she could come, but only if she put up and shut up. He also admitted, after all those years of arguing and searching for the truth about Sharron and the illegitimate child, that he did have an affair with her and he did have another son.

My father had so many affairs, but that one was the one that she had always held up to the light of being utterly intolerable to her. I suppose we all draw the line to our limits in some way; perhaps it allowed her to negotiate why she allowed all the other affairs. 'Yes, I put up with all the other affairs, but if I find out Phillip slept with Sharon, I will leave,' I imagined her saying. In truth, my mother couldn't leave, not in the way she'd imagine, boots on, like the song said, start walkin'. Her childhood of abandonment, her trauma bonding and her staunch identity as the archetype of a martyr deemed it impossible. So, my mother got drunk, got into her Mercedes and drove her car to the Lions Gate Bridge with the intention of slamming on the accelerator and flying off the side into the bay below.

Once there, however, she realised it wasn't high enough to guarantee she would die, she might just end up paralysed and Dad would just leave her behind, so she drove back home. When Father returned from work that night, she agreed to move to The Bahamas. He presented her with a very beautiful ring in exchange for her accepting his affair. She saw that as an acknowledgement of the one time in her life she confronted him and stood up.

She gave me that ring years later when telling me that story and told me it was to always remind me to stand up; she made me promise to do so with any man, even if I was still in love, no matter what. I promised.

I moved full-time to The Bahamas with my parents. Our first house was the green house, not because the outside was green but because the inside was. It had been pre-decorated by a top designer, which made my mother roar with laughter when viewing it. It was garish with its shiny silver vases and light fixtures, big green

pillows with frogs on them and stark yellow curtains. I discovered
the reason for the frog theme one day when showering. Naked
and washing my hair, I noticed a rather large frog in the corner
of my shower. I love all creatures, so I said out loud, 'Well, hello
there, little fellow.' The next thing I know, this massive frog leaps
at me and suctions onto my hand. I screamed and tried in vain to
furiously shake it off, but it rode my hand like a bull rider. Finally,
my sister Keily, who was visiting, ran in and ripped it off my hand.
The upside of living on the canal was having one's yacht moored;
the downside was the canal was riddled with large frogs.

Keily and I had a lot of fun when she visited. We would dress
up at night, wait until our parents were asleep and I'd drive my
mother's car down the winding road to Paradise Island where we
would dance all night at the discos. The key was to make sure you
threw out the receipt from paying the bridge toll onto the island
and getting home before 6:30 am. I can't tell you how many times
I'd be racing my father, him in his Mercedes, me in my mother's
BMW, neck to neck, trying to get home before him. He would
be sneaking out all night, too, gambling and seeing mistresses or
prostitutes. Father loved a good game, so without words spoken, we
learned if we got home before him, even within seconds, nothing
would happen.

If he got home first, he would say he was up all night worried
about us and wake our mother, dob us in and we would be
punished. Of all the games, however, that one at least was fun, most
of the time.

We loved going out to the discos. There would be competitions
every night and I would win most of them. Bottles of champagne or
vouchers for dinner, it was never about the prize. I loved dance-offs

and the exhilaration of the crowd cheering me on and the applause. Dance-offs were about expression, fun, entertainment, respect and talent. I didn't drink a lot, but when I did, I'd have Long Island iced teas or Campari with grapefruit.

I remember a few nights stumbling to the car, laughing hysterically with Keily as we flopped into our seats. I'd drive those winding dark roads along the ocean like a race car driver. In those days, very few people lived in The Bahamas full time, so the roads were always empty, the only risk was driving off the road onto the beach, but even then, it would be an easy recovery. We would laugh about the different experiences we had in that way only sisters can, like the time Keily slept with one of the break-dancers only to discover he was making those same break-dancing moves during sex; we laughed hysterically about that. Then there was the time our very religious maid came into our rooms when we were getting ready to go to the disco and said, 'You're all gonna die in a fiery crash on the way back from the disco 'cause you're all sinners.' I answered, 'Thank you, Thelma, bless you too,' then laughed from the sheer horror. Those nights of sneaking out eventually came to an end, however, when I forgot to throw the toll bridge receipt out and Mother found it in the car. After that, Father would remove the distributor cap from her car and Keily and I had no choice but to stay home.

Things weren't going very well at home, they never really were, but this seemed worse. Father was with his mistresses more than ever and wasn't even trying to hide them. 'I'm going to my boat and my girlfriends will be joining me,' he would mandate.

Then the catalyst for my mother finally leaving my father happened. I was standing inside the lounge area where the large

French doors looked out onto the pool area. Mother was standing by the side of the pool, a drink in her hand and clearly teetering back and forth from drunkenness. Father didn't have a drink and although he was likely also drinking, he seemed quite aware. He walked up to my mother and suddenly pushed her into the pool with great force. It happened so fast that I stood frozen. It felt like I was watching a movie in slow motion. Mother had an extreme phobia to water over her head since she had almost drowned as a child and Father knew this.

I watched motionless as Mother was disoriented, underwater, ripples of water churning from the chaos of her panicking, somersaulting underneath; she seemed disorientated. Why doesn't she just grab onto the ladder? I wondered. What startled me the most, however, was the haunting expression on my father's face while he just stood there, calmly looking around, his eyes darting back and forth, his body not even flinching or motioning to help. Instead, he looked down at her drowning in the pool. He had the same expression on his face I'd seen when he won at the tables, gambling, a clever, wry grin of how lucky he was. I imagined he knew at that moment that if she drowned, he would get away with it. I wanted to scream, but at the same time, I was paralysed and in complete shock at how calm and aware he was. I wanted to believe he would suddenly reach out; I needed to believe he would save her. Surely he didn't really want her dead?'

In that moment, those seconds, time and I froze. I witnessed my father in his limitless capabilities. I learned there is no bottom to Cluster B, we only need to believe there is for our own safety and sanity. He was looking around to make sure no one else was watching, not knowing I was standing in the living room, in front of the large sliding glass doors. My mouth was so tight it locked, I tried to make a sound, but I just felt the sounds buried in my belly as stifled, muffled cries. My ten-year-old self was standing there again, the gun pointed at my forehead, watching, needing my mum. Suddenly my mother's arm started reaching out from the water like she was grasping for a lifeline, anything to save her, until she grabbed hold of the railing on the steel ladder, lifting herself up out of the water enough to gasp much-needed air. She coughed and sputtered, then took in an enormous inhalation. She looked at my father like a deer caught in the headlights. At that moment, we all knew what had almost just happened. My mother got to live that day.

Chapter Eleven
The Penthouse
Age 16–21

Separated, Mother did as she always promised and brought me with her to live in her new penthouse on the 15th floor in North Vancouver, Canada. Father was left behind in the house on the canal in The Bahamas with his yacht, his millions, his cigarettes, his alcohol and his three mistresses, not including the prostitutes. She finally left him. I'd dreamt of this moment and replayed it so often in my mind; it was the beginning of hope for my mother and me. I was filled with so many ideas and plans for our future, especially hers. I was present to bear witness at the airport as my parents said goodbye. My father cried, at least I think that's what it was supposed to be, as his face grimaced, but I didn't actually see any tears. My mother's eyes were too clouded by her tsunami of emotions, she wouldn't have been able to tell the difference. The contradiction of their catastrophic coupling and their devastation at being parted felt like a strange time to show such dramatics, just as the gates to leave permanently opened. I suspected then it was orchestrated to imprint doubt, plant a festering seed that in time would grow to rekindle, rebind and rewrite the spell that kept her bound to him.

Mother didn't cope with her time without my father. Instead of rising, healing and rebuilding, she sank further than she ever did into the drinking. Passing out became so commonplace I'd often walk past her, seemingly oblivious. I saw her peripherally and I cared so much that the pain was at times unbearable to face, so sometimes I just didn't; I just kept walking. She always woke up by morning only to end up in the exact same position, just in a different place. If she wasn't passed out on the couch, it would be the chair or the floor, an empty vodka bottle lying next to her, pants soiled; it was our normal. Except for that one day I came home when I was supposed to sleep over at Joachim's.

I met Joachim at a club when I borrowed my mother's blue silk dress. I snuck out with my friend at the time and lied about my age to the doorman. We went to the Greek café first for tapas and free glasses of wine as Nikos flirted terribly with me despite him being a forty-something married man. Feeling tipsy and excited to go to the local club, we were sweating bullets as we lined up, waiting for the doorman to approve our IDs. This tall, clean-shaven, blonde man with a chiselled chin and a strong German accent introduced himself to me. He was chatting with me as we walked closer to the bouncer, seemingly a regular, he vouched for us and we went in. It was another world inside; the dancer in me felt an instant chemical rush. Lights, disco ball, dance music, I just had to get out on that floor and move. We hung out all night with Joachim, who bought us drinks and had genuine care for our welfare.

He was kind, extremely intelligent and oblivious to our young plan until the club closed. After that, we went to Denny's, a popular restaurant that served a twenty-four-hour breakfast. We were all sitting at the table eating and drinking coffee when Joachim started asking us about where we lived and if we needed a ride home. It was at that moment my friend and I just balked in shock, suddenly realising we did not finalise our plan and still had hours to hang out before we could walk home. We did the old, I'm sleeping at her house routine but hadn't considered it was still only three a.m. Joachim caught on and I eventually confessed I was only sixteen and he did his best to hang out with us until the sun was up. Of course, we got caught and got a good lashing of verbal abuse, but we were happy never to do that again as it was all too exhausting and hard in the end.

Joachim, however, became my first boyfriend. He wined and dined me, philosophised with me, taught me how to mix ketchup with mayonnaise to make a shrimp cocktail sauce and asked me if I knew 'For whom the bell tolls?' It took me years to figure that one out, but of course, it's from Ernest Hemingway's novel *For whom the Bell Tolls* and the answer, in short, is 'It Tolls for Thee.'

Chris was home visiting one evening when the Volkswagen Joachim drove stopped outside our home and I got my first kiss goodnight. Chris woke me up at three a.m. raging that I was a slut and a whore and Joachim was a coward and a perpetrator. It was beyond his normal protective demeanour, it was abuse. I was shocked and confused, but I also saw his rage as jealousy and control. He had always been overly protective, but this felt wrong. I saw more signs of those conflicting behaviours in Chris. The lines of brother and sister felt blurred, at least for him it seemed.

Joachim and I dated long enough for him to see and experience the dysfunctions in my family. So, the first time he invited me to sleep over at his house, I accepted and left my mother alone in the penthouse. I was enjoying a swim in the pool at Joachim's house but something didn't feel right. I felt a rush of panic in my gut and in my mind I saw my mother dead. I told Joachim I had to go back home, that something wasn't right and I felt she was in danger. He offered to come up with me, but I wanted to go alone. Shame makes you want to hide those kinds of things.

Once the elevator doors opened onto the fifteenth floor, I smelt burnt toast. I quickly opened the door and to my left was my mother, an empty vodka bottle on the floor next to the couch she was passed out on, her pants soiled. Smoke was billowing out of the kitchen; it was already clouding the living room and into the entrance hall I was standing in. I rushed into the kitchen and opened the oven as flames leapt toward me. I grabbed the extinguisher and put the fire out, then opened every window. Everything was executed with complete calm and precision, as if I was trained. I was training my entire life for crisis and all you have in those moments is to stay alert, in control and logical if you want to survive. The aftermath, however, is the crash.

That sudden adrenaline surge, the emotions, the burdens, the fears, the lack of expression and reconciliation depletes everything you are. I went to bed and slept for hours.

The next day we talked about what happened. Mother promised, as she always did, to stop drinking, get help and make the changes she needed to. She would be so remorseful and cry and promise me everything. After a time, however, I realised her promises, however hopeful, were just lies, unreality, lack of accountability, denial, pain, fear, low self-worth, encoding and part of the cycle.

Father moved back into the penthouse. He kept the house in The Bahamas as the plan was to eventually go there again, but for now, he was home. He was discussing my future and insisting I take a business secretary course to prepare myself to earn some money. The last thing I wanted to do was business secretary school, but within days of his return, I was enrolled and managing public school and business school. I had to leave boarding school as Mother couldn't be left alone and life was becoming more and more uncertain each day. I didn't do as well at public school. I found the chaos at home, the sterility of the impersonal classrooms and a group of children I didn't know and didn't connect to lonely. By this time, I just wanted real, normal, genuine people who could just be my friend. I needed love, calm and consistency. I was lucky I did have a small group of friends from elementary school and my boarding school days that were all those things; they were my lifeline more than they ever knew. I would spend time with them or write letters, but at public school, I felt alone. It's a faded memory of a painful and complicated time and I'm happy to keep it as such. Like anything your subconscious keeps as a faded memory, it is doing so to protect you; let it.

I arrived home after business secretary school to my father drinking his whiskey on ice in the crystal tumbler. As I walked in, he said, 'I was very angry today; do you know that?'

'No,' I replied, confused.

'I called your business secretary school because I assumed you would be failing. You know what they said?'

'No.'

'They said you are the top student, you are excelling and you are extremely hard working. Can you believe that?'

'No,' I said like a trained seal. To have said, 'Of course I know I'm doing well' or even just 'Yes' could have flicked a switch, so staying meek was always the best course of action. It's how we were trained to honour him. To my surprise, he was thrilled and said he was amazed and happy I was doing so well.

There weren't many moments our father praised us or validated our successes, but when he did, we felt elation. Maybe now Father will be happy, maybe he's trying, maybe if I keep doing well and laying low, we will all be OK, maybe?

I was out with Chris shopping one afternoon not long after when he decided to come up to the penthouse to see Mother and Father. It was a great day, sunny, we were laughing and everything was just so positive. It was only around three in the afternoon, so we didn't expect what would happen next when we opened the door to the apartment. Father was gutted, absolutely smashed on whiskey. He had his crystal tumbler in his hand, the ice cubes were crashing against his glass and he staggered, which took a lot for my father. Chris walked in ahead of me. Father lunged at him, his mouth wet from whiskey, and raged, 'YOU'RE AN ASSHOLE. DID YOU HEAR ME? YOU'RE AN ASSHOLE, A FUCKING, ASSHOLE, ASSHOLE, ASSHOLE.'

Chris was tearing up and his body was rigid; he looked like a statue frozen in place, petrified and trapped. I said, 'STOP, STOOOP, you're hurting him. He didn't do anything. Stop it. Please stop it.' But he wouldn't stop. He fired those words like verbal bullets, pelting him so close to his face and body he had nothing to guard his already fragile psyche.

Then I saw it. My brother broke that day. It was in his eyes; his bright blue, soulful eyes clouded over and there was this disconnect like a plug was ripped out of the wall. The light that used to always shine from behind those beautiful eyes that cast a soft hue now looked dull and in time, pain and rage loomed behind them. He broke him.

This intelligent, creative, beautiful man who was trying so hard to keep his mind intact cracked. I looked at my father and said, 'FUCK YOU!' I bolted up the stairs a millisecond after saying it. I could feel his breath on my neck and his thick hands grasping at me as I ran as fast as I could. My dancer's thighs saved me as I got into my bathroom and locked the door just as I saw the handle moving downward. I was safe behind that bathroom door by the width of a hair. I exhaled. The adrenaline in me was so high I just sat there for hours, not even feeling the time. I knew if I came out, anything could happen.

The next morning there was a knock at the door; it was my mother telling me it was safe to come out. She sat me on the bed and said, 'You know your father was so upset yesterday. He drank and cried all night. He was devastated because he said if he had caught you, he would have thrown you off the fifteenth floor to your death. He saw red and it scared him because he said he almost killed you.'

I remember thinking, 'Um, am I supposed to feel concerned for him? Almost killing me?' I had nothing more to say. There was nothing to be said. In the typical pattern of my father, I was kicked out. I was sixteen and I had to get out because I almost made him kill me. I cried, 'But I'm only sixteen. Where am I supposed to go?' It did nothing to prevent Father from kicking me out and so within a night, I found myself living in an old apartment in a small four-storey building in the red-light district of downtown Vancouver.

The first night in my apartment, I watched a young man check every car in the car park in front of my building until he finally got into one and promptly stole it. I'd never seen anything like that, nor the prostitutes that worked on every corner either. I found a job at a real estate company but had no idea what work was. I didn't do very well as I spent far too much time going to the cafeteria, sampling every snack and trying to hide my dishes in the bottom drawer of my desk. My boss smelt the collection of dishes and opened the drawer, giving me an embarrassing warning. He should have fired me, but it turned out my father had called them, having used their services many times for his business, and forced them to give me a job. It made sense as I had absolutely no skills in that industry.

I met a group of Polish refugees at the local pub and became very close with all of them. They would invite me most nights to their place, a twenty-minute walk from where I lived. We would drink, share bread, play music and laugh. They were the most intriguing, funniest and most loving people I'd ever met. One night after walking home, a man was standing outside my building looking very angry. He looked like a bikie, weathered, tough and he was waiting for me. 'Do you realise how dangerous it is walking home every night, a young, pretty girl like you? I grew up on these streets and I understand them, but you are a lamb to the wolves. From now on, if you want to go visit your friend and walk home at three a.m., you tell me and I will walk you back and forth every night, but you are not doing it alone.'

I was shocked this rough-looking man was so kind and genuine and sure enough, he did walk me back and forth. I could never remember his name or whether he even told me, but I will always remember him and so many other people during those years of my life. Somehow, I was being looked after, watched, protected and guided. I always felt the synchronicity of something bigger than me, making sure I was OK. It created a balance of the constant battles of life that somehow destiny was trying to keep swinging me toward something greater. I have always carried that belief shrouded in humility and gratitude. That same man called me on my landline phone one night and said, 'Hey, it's snowing.' I rushed excitedly to my window, saying, 'No way?' as it was still summer, but I felt disheartened and confused when I saw outside was dry and warm. I didn't get his sense of humour but learnt years later that 'snowing' was code for cocaine. He was inviting me downstairs for cocaine. It highlights how young and innocent I was, a lamb to the wolves indeed.

Mother and Father were moving back to The Bahamas. After a home robbery and feeling lost with no real sense of direction, I said yes to their offer to come along. I was happy with my decision at first. I lived in the pool cabana, I ate breakfast by the pool, served by the maid every morning, I danced at the discos most nights, I water skied past Julio Iglesias' house, snorkelled and hung out with incredible friends.

Some of my friends had parents who were lords and ladies, some were famous authors or famous political families, but I also had friends who were local Bahamians who didn't have a lot of money but were emotionally and spiritually wealthy—the best kind. I remember seeing Stephanie, the Princess of Monaco, walking on the beach in Lyford Cay after the car crash in which her mother died. She was with the rest of her family and the grief on their faces was understandably palpable. Famous people were commonplace as most had one of several holiday homes there. My father was excited when Sean Connery came aboard our boat, they had drinks together and my father joked he would never wash his hand again after shaking his.

I was very close to two young men, Henry and Michael, whose father was a very famous author. Mother said the rumour was his wife tolerated his many affairs as he said he needed them to build the stories of his characters. Henry would invite me to his cabana, adjacent to his family home, for vanilla ice cream with Kahlua. Not being able to manage alcohol very well, it was an enticing elixir that made the room dreamy and his kisses made me want to keep coming back for more; until he came over for dinner one night. I was in the bathroom combing my hair when he walked in, opened my make-up bag and pulled the mascara out. He brushed his lashes until they were dark black and very full and then fluttered them at me while we sat at the dinner table. We knew at that moment why we were destined to just stay friends. He was gay. In fact, it was my brother who started to go over to Henry's cabana most nights when he would visit. He told me at that time, he was interested in men and seemed very comfortable with that as his choice. Chris and I often went to discos together and he would question me on which guy I fancied; he always liked the men with nice bums and swaying hips. He loved watching them dance.

Whether Chris was gay, bi or curious wasn't ever an issue for me, nor would it have been for any of his siblings. Although no doubt Father would have used it wildly against him. Chris had enormous concerns about that. He feared being written out of the will and completely abandoned. It's hard to describe how intense abandonment is to someone who has had it held up over their head as the absolute proof of one's unworthiness; it's lethal.

Chris was on his own journey after having very close and connected relationships with women, especially his first love, Sandra, at Princeton. She was extremely athletic, lean, an equestrian racehorse rider, brilliant, funny, very family oriented and she deeply loved my brother. Her short hair and lean, muscular body gave her an androgynous look at the time; perhaps that mattered, perhaps it didn't. I know Chris was madly in love with her because he talked about her to me all the time. They were young and after several years they broke up. It was sudden, initiated by Chris and yet he didn't handle it well. He had so many things going on at once, namely feeling betrayed by our father, and it was haunting him.

He left Princeton and took off to Greece, where he stayed for several years. Chris slept with women and men while away, but once back in Los Angeles, he lived for several years in committed relationships with two different men. I never knew much about the first one, but the second one worked as a voiceover actor and used to leave the funniest messages on their voice answering machine.

Relationships ending seemed to disarm Chris, so when those relationships ended, he moved to Vancouver. I worried about his decision as he had told me some of his friends in Vancouver were homophobic. He was also worried our father would disinherit him if he ever knew about his relationships with men. I wondered then if his decisions after that, to completely shut off any aspect of his life with men, contributed to the other wounds he carried about never being enough. I remember calling him at that time and asking him if his new girlfriend knew about his relationships with men. He completely ignored the question. So, I left it be. Chris said he was happy and in love with a woman, so I was happy for him too. My only worry was the risk to him if he had to cut off a part of who he was. Those parts within us that get exiled can fester and rebel with disturbing destruction.

The unacceptance of any part of him was always the constant abuse projected from Father. Chris was born perfect, in fact, exceptional. Had all those parts been supported, celebrated, nurtured, loved, heard, seen, valued and elevated, my brother was destined to stand out in a crowd. Nurture will always be the greatest predictor of every adult we ultimately raise.

We were sitting on our boat in Vancouver and Chris' new girlfriend was on his lap, unusual for all of us as public displays of affection were not encouraged. I was so elated to see him, as it had been a while since we caught up. He took me aside and said, 'If my girlfriend likes you, you're in; if she doesn't, you're out.' I roared with laughter at the absurdity. Chris and I were inseparable, I thought. I was wrong. After that meet-up, I didn't see my brother for over thirty years.

Back in The Bahamas, I spent time with the many friends I made who lived outside of Lyford Cay. I met most of them through dancing or associations. My Black friends, however, were allegedly causing a problem with the neighbour next door to us. An American couple lived there and they trained their German Shepherd to bark at and attack Black people. It was a rather bizarre thing to do while living in a mostly Black populated country, I thought. One day a group of my friends, who happened to all be Black, came over for a swim. We had the best day as any young adults would, swimming, laughing, all just normal fun. My father came home enraged as our neighbours reported to the council that they were very concerned that I spoke to Black people, hung out with Black people and danced with Black people.

My mother, following the orders of my father, organised for me to go on a trip with a group of white kids to sort me out. The first thing the next morning, I was booked on the mail boat. Notorious for sinking, as its owner built it out of whatever wood they could muster, I hesitantly went aboard and travelled to the island of Eleuthera. It is a beautiful island off the mainland known for magnificent long white beaches and crystal-clear water. I was excited at its beauty but confused as I sat in a cabin with five other white young adults. I found it odd that I should immediately feel an alliance with these people by the sheer association of our skin colour. It was the most illogical, racist and abhorrent concept to me and I was disappointed my mother was following through with those orders as I knew they weren't values she upheld. I tried to get to know the white kids but to be frank, I found them pretentious, racist and entitled just because their families had money. That kind of bought elitism never made sense to me. I always felt respect should be earned and found most people without money far outweighed class, integrity and generosity. The only boy in that group who seemed nice was Dutch and he lived on the island. It was clear from the start that a coupling was forming and everyone had intentions to hook up. I wasn't feeling that at all and wanted to leave, but the mail boat only ran once each morning, so I was stuck.

As the night wore on, the Dutch boy told funny stories like why half his bum cheek was missing. Apparently, a shark bit it off. He was wild, tanned, funny and clearly paired with me. I wasn't even remotely interested, so after only one glass of rum, I went to bed. I woke up with that very drunk Dutch guy on top of me. I tried to push him off; I think I succeeded several times, but I don't remember much. I know he had sex with me, I know I didn't want it, I know I said no and tried to push him off, I know he felt heavy when he was on top of me, I know I was alone and everyone else was passed out, I know I froze, I know I don't remember and somehow the details blew away, like the wind to sand.

I wasn't hurt physically and I never even considered what that was, but I was angry. The next day I got on that mail boat and cried the whole way back while I ate an entire box of vanilla wafers. I remember that in fine detail; the taste of salt from the sea spray kept landing on my biscuit. My mother met me at the docks and when I got off I said, 'Happy? Your white kids were dreadful. It was utterly horrific.' She never asked why, but she also never challenged me about my choice of friends again.

My Bahamian friends were my family. We danced and laughed; they even took me in between apartments after I finally left home and lived on my own. I turned to my Bahamian family for the love and consistency I craved. They gave it to me in abundance. I remember every time I'd go to Iris' house she would ask me for my lunch order. Knowing she didn't have a lot of money, I'd always say a tuna sandwich and a Coke. Sure enough, I got that every time. What I didn't know was Iris would take away that portion of the money or food meant to feed her eight kids and grandkids. I was always treated as a priority. Once

I knew that I would try to insist I wasn't hungry, but she would never fall for that. She would also make fresh bread on an old clay stove, cook chicken souse and conch fritters and bring in a large tub filled with warm water for me to bathe in. She would roar with laughter when I screamed every time a rat ran over my foot while watching TV, which happened a lot. Iris was proud of her home made of cement brick that in itself was status in those days over the plywood most homes were made of. Iris was married and had eight kids, but her husband died young from diabetes. She worked as a maid for years and raised her kids with love, a firm hand and as much food as she could get. All her kids were talented, kind, funny, loving and welcoming of me. Up until I was well in my thirties, I would still get little envelopes in the mail with money for each of my children. Iris showed me another way that life can be happy and that family does exist, food matters and home isn't about money; it's love, it's a connection, it's a choice we can all create.

I was travelling back and forth to Montreal to visit my sisters as Father wanted me to consider moving to Canada. He didn't see any potential for me long-term in The Bahamas. I had tried to find dancing opportunities, but the only gig at that time was to be a showgirl. I did try out and I got a position, but since it was topless, my father said, 'Over my dead body.' He visited those shows and those girls with his business partners, but he couldn't have his daughter in the line-up. So, I got a job as an aesthetician. I was trained by Helena Rubinstein and managed a top spa on Paradise Island. Again, I was terrible at my job. I would slap a hot towel onto the client's face and refuse to squeeze their blackheads. When asked to wax the hairs by their privates, I shuddered at the thought and simply walked away.

Rather than sell the eighty-dollar vials of cow sperm to the women for their wrinkles, I suggested they could get their boyfriends to ejaculate on their faces for free. Needless to say, I wasn't meant for that job. However, I was a massive success. I had a large clientele of mostly prostitutes who saw me regularly; they even tipped me twenty dollars. I honestly thought I was amazing until one day, a young girl who prostituted for a living said, 'Deirdre, you're the worst aesthetician ever.' I shamelessly acted shocked and looked perplexed. She then explained, 'You're terrible at being an aesthetician. That's not why all the girls come to you. You are an incredible listener; you don't judge us and you give amazing advice. You should be a therapist; the girls all call you their therapist.' That moment changed my life. It seems my journey, my mother's influence and those night-time confessionals created innate skills that I could use. It felt right. I found my purpose.

Not long after that conversation, I found out I was pregnant. I wanted to have a child. My priorities in life were children first, marriage second and a career third. I suppose my lifestyle at that time gave me a much different position and therefore influenced my choices. We were all on trust funds by then, fifteen hundred US dollars a month to begin with, then three thousand a month and then five thousand a month. The money we received was loaded with complexities as it was generous and we felt grateful, but it also created a dependency that caused a deeper sickness in my siblings. It became our father's greatest power over us, the gravy train we called it.

My beautiful daughter was born in Nassau, The Bahamas.
My doctor, Dr Churro, was an African doctor who used
wooden instruments to listen to my baby's development. I was
prescheduled for a caesarean, as was the protocol in The Bahamas.
Some said since I was white, they knew I'd likely pay the five
thousand US dollar fee. I woke up in the hospital with absolutely
no pain medication, it was excruciating, but I was blissfully happy
and I was in love as I looked at my beautiful daughter.

My parents stayed away for the birth as they were not happy
I was romantically involved with a man of colour. I thought they
just needed time to reset, but a few weeks after my daughter was
born, my father called to invite me for breakfast. I was elated. He
never invited me for breakfast; it must be to celebrate the great
news that they were now grandparents. Once seated at our table,
my father, Mother by his side, passed me a yellow file. They
explained their little trip to Miami was to organise a fast adoption
and that I had a chance to live my life and no one would have
to know. Mother looked down as he spoke, I knew she wanted
nothing to do with it, being adopted out herself, but she was so
controlled and deemed powerless, albeit self-appointed by now. I
stood up, shattered and disgusted. 'I planned my baby,' I said and
walked off.

I was appalled at their insanity, hypocrisy, audacity,
abhorrent elitist rhetoric and their failings at parenting and now
grandparenting. No dysfunction warranted that injury to one of
my greatest blessings in life.

I didn't know it then, but that was no more or no less about
the actual reason they put forth. My father's patterns were never
really about racism, elitism or whatever his gaslighting dictated; it

was about control. Having children and having a partner meant I was less pliable and accessible and he owned us.

I eventually moved to Montreal, Canada, where I had my second blessing, my son, and then married the father to my children. My parents didn't come to our wedding; it wasn't much as we didn't have a lot of money at that time. A gold ring with diamond dust, I wore a salmon-coloured dress with shoulder pads and he wore a shiny black suit. My sister Keily was my witness and his brother Rod was his. After the simple ceremony, which took convincing as it was with a Catholic priest and we had only just met him a few weeks before, we went home to share a store-bought cake with his mother and our small children. It was perfect.

Rudy is a tall, muscular Black man who worked as a welder, cooked Caribbean food like a trained chef and did his best to create the best life for us all. I loved his rawness to life, his resourcefulness and his hard-working values toward life and family. For years we were the perfect family, or at least we tried to be.

We lived a great life of working out, dancing, music, great food, lots of friends and doing everything with our children; I had my forever family. It lasted a long time; however, things became complicated. As I progressed in my studies and career, he felt pangs of jealousy which, in time, created arguments. He had wounds, I had wounds, my therapeutic studies hadn't kicked in yet, our arguments slowly became toxic and we had no choice but to divorce. It took a few years to process the ending of our marriage, as I think we both held such hopes of breaking the cycles in our families and so wanted to have that perfect marriage we both craved so deeply. But we were young.

Our friendship, however, lasted and to this day, we are bonded
by our mutual love and respect for our children and for what
we both tried to create when we were still very young. He also
graciously took the time and space to take me aside many years
ago to acknowledge and apologise for the fights that escalated
into threats and abuse. We sealed the wounds of our coupling
with mutual respect and love toward our youth, our lessons, our
growth and most importantly, the shared bond and deep love of
our children.

At the time we parted, I had been studying at college doing
my three-year diploma in Social (Psychology) Counselling.
It was a requirement then to do twenty hours a week in work
placement per term as part of the curriculum. By the completion
of my studies, I had accumulated over eight thousand hours
of placement in everything from homelessness, group homes,
schizophrenia, death and dying, Holocaust survivors, cancer
survivors, peer mentoring, community outreach, sexual assault
and addictions. After college, I was accepted into McGill
University for a Bachelor of Social Work, which I completed in
three years but transferred into a small, independent college that
accepted my credits to date. I wasn't coping at university. The
abnormal psychology was heightening my post-traumatic stress
disorder, triggering all my still-fresh memories of my parent's
alcoholism and all that came with it. Besides, the information
being provided at that time sounded wrong to me. According to
the teachings at that time, alcoholism was deemed genetic and
guaranteed to be inherited by the next generation. It followed the
inheritable disease theory, which frustrated me. I wasn't going to

be an alcoholic and I knew I had the power to make that choice. I was triggered by the enabling of unburdening my parents with any accountability and deeming them powerless. I believed in a healing process of hope, possibility, nurture over nature, a strong stance on accountability, truth and a mind-body approach. Added to these concerns is that it coincided with Michael's death.

I'd been dating Michael long-distance for a little over four years, as he lived in New York. We met on a trip to Jamaica and he pursued me most days, inviting me to a bar or restaurant. I wouldn't go and so he would just try again. I was away on my own, one of only a few vacations I took without my children. He was a kind man and very persistent. Finally, on his last night, he walked into the hotel lounge and just said, 'Hey, this is my last night, I really like you and clearly I've been pursuing you, but could we just chat for a bit?' I said OK, as he was so soft-spoken and kind and seemed very genuine. We chatted about all kinds of things that night. He was highly intelligent, an editor at *The Wall Street Journal,* head of the Dow Jones multimedia group, an avid jazz music lover, funny and so humble and sweet. It felt magical and connected.

We walked down to the beach with our wine and he pulled a tiny speaker out of his bag and played jazz music under the stars. He gave me his business card and I gave him my address, which is what we did back then to communicate. Once home, I wrote him a card about really feeling a beautiful connection. On the day he received it, he called me just as I also received a card from him saying the same thing. I flew to New York to see him one weekend and our love dove into an intensity of what felt like destined soulmates. It was a profound love, a beautiful love, a love that felt secure and inspiring. He was my forever. Michael taught me how to love deeply, honestly and with a raw, open and transcendent chemistry. We communicated a lot with music and he often played 'For the cool in you'.

I was home one night when I had a strange compulsion to call Michael. I had already been calling him every day for the last four years, but this felt different, like a panicked compulsion. He didn't answer and even as time went by, he didn't call back, which was highly unusual for him. It was night-time and I still hadn't heard from him. I remember writing something in my journal about the ominous night skies in The Bahamas and the kaleidoscope perspective of life. It was an automatic writing moment, where no thoughts passed through me as the words just glided across the paper. It wasn't until the next morning that I read it and fully felt it. I got chills reading it as if hearing it for the first time. Something was wrong. Then the phone rang. It was Michael's brother from Cleveland, a busy cardiologist whom I had never met nor spoken to.

'Hi, Deirdre. Is Michael there with you?'

My heart sank as I said no.

'Oh no, I was hoping he was. I will get back to you.'

I have no idea how long I waited by that phone; minutes, hours, shock created such a blur. The acceleration of my pounding heart blocked my ears as I waited. The phone rang.

'Deirdre, Michael is dead...'

I dropped the phone and ran out the door and across the schoolyard. I ran until I completely unfolded, knees on the ground and wailed a bellowing primal cry for the catastrophic loss of my love. Death, especially the first one, is so all-encompassing.

We think as we sit on our couches at home that we will handle it with such grace. I, with my comparative religious and spiritual studies, begged Allah, Christ, Buddha and anyone I could think of for a lifeline to hold me in those moments.

At the funeral, I realised everyone was comforting each other, mothers to sons, husbands to wives, partners to partners, friends or colleagues to each other, but I stood alone. My support, my love, was being buried. He was placed in a wall at the entrance. I'd never seen that before; it was all so sterile and it felt so lonely. But I did feel him all around me.

Leading up to the funeral, I arrived in New York without one piece of black clothing to my name. The wife of his best friend took me shopping. While standing in the shop, staring blankly at a rack of clothing, an employee who looked very similar to Michael asked, 'Are you OK?' Now, this is New York, so I was surprised and said, 'No, my fiancé died and I'm here to buy an outfit for his funeral.' He immediately walked behind me and wrapped his arms tightly from behind to give me a hug. I was taken by surprise as that was the unique way Michael hugged me. Then he said in my ear, 'He is here with you in different forms, but he's here, you'll know.'

There is no timeframe to grieve; recovering from Michael's death took me ten years. Of course, to the outside world, I was functioning fine as life went on, but inside, I was not in my body in the way that I know feels like me. I integrated that grief into my spiritual studies, healing arts, dance, running, music, the deep love and gift of my children and the messages it taught me that had a deeply profound impact on the direction of what and where I studied and the choices I made in life.

My mother apologised to me for naming me Deirdre, the goddess of sorrows, and felt the legacy of my name was to blame. The story says a witch approached a mother carrying a girl named Deirdre. She would have powers and beauty and therefore they should hide her in the woods as Deirdre would bring sorrow to any man who loved her. As she grew into a beautiful, fair woman, the king and his knights rode through the woods and saw her. The king, besotted, approached and requested she ride back with him, but she refused. It was a knight who caught her eye as she did his. He came back for her and they began an affair and fell deeply in love. The king heard of their coupling and requested they come to the castle. The knight agreed as his honour was in question. Once there, the king had the knight killed. Deirdre laid on top of him and died of a broken heart. Still jealous, the king buried them on either side of the river, but a tree grew on each side that had vines that reached across to each other, forming an archway, as nothing could ever keep them apart. I love my name and that story. It speaks to the deeply romantic person I am at heart and unburdens me with that plight as, after all, it's the legacy of my namesake.

I have learned from love lost and love betrayed 'forever after' is an illusion. I have lived many lives in this one life and therefore embrace my 'forever right now'. From that, I will always feel loved.

I worked hard after Michael's death as I intuitively knew my only options were to fight or die young under the cumulative pains that weighed me down. From a study perspective, it was alarmingly clear the pathway of studying toward being a therapist at that time was a linear, clinical approach and only studying the spiritual, alternative modalities lacked the theoretical support needed. I felt a combination of it all was the only way to address the full spectrum of mind, body and spirit healing.

One does not grieve with just the mind and the body takes much longer. Michael's death encouraged me to leave McGill University and transfer to a smaller independent school that offered an emphasis on Jungian psychology infused with hypnotherapy, neuro-linguistic therapy, music therapy, dream analysis, energy work, mindfulness, parts therapy, family systems and many other modalities taught by doctors, researchers, professors and headed by my mentors Dr Marilyn Rossner, a child behaviourist and well-known medium, and her husband Dr John Rossner, head of the department of Religious studies at Concordia University. I was didactically healing not just those grieving parts of Michael but facing the wounds of my childhood.

Most of those wounds were best stroked with a logical brush, but for all those loose ends that left wounds with no way of experiencing reconciliation, the Eastern philosophies and spiritual principles invited me to imagine, create, express and re-enact through symbolism, ritual, visualisations, mindfulness and philosophical contemplations, inciting a deeper embodied approach.

That was the kind of therapy I believed in, that I was developing and integrating into my own methods and one I knew from my own childhood with my mother and influence from her spiritual and psychological intervention worked.

Michael taught me how to love, the power of humility, to follow that road less travelled, that my strength was his favourite part about me and that I carried it in the kindest person he knew. He called me a beautiful mass of contradictions. His love filled the gaps my father created with the hope and healing only true love can give. Time, therefore, doesn't matter, as in our short four years together, he elevated me into more, so much beautiful more.

Of course, my history encoded me to unconsciously choose a man that would challenge my wounds. I met that man I deemed my soulmate and I was ready to dive in deep again. Michael made that look so safe, and besides, it's the motto I chose to live by: live life at full throttle. So, I jumped, rather leapt, into this beautiful man. He swept me off my feet and made my heart flutter every time he walked into the room. That itself made it worth it, regardless of the outcome.

It felt like an old-world love, enchanting, deep, chemically charged; he mirrored everything I needed and craved, if only I knew it was all strategic then. Schema therapy says I had no hope and my destiny psychologically was always to end up partnered with Mr Cluster B. The goal, of course, is to get a watered down version of my father, regardless of his wounds. If he became a better man because of loving me, I, too, would heal all my deepest wounds. The risk, however, is Mr Cluster B could also tear them wide open. I got the latter.

I saw signs early on, but he wasn't the over-the-top kind, or at least I hadn't seen it. I hadn't studied the covert type yet, so he managed to fall through the cracks.

While I was with him, I gained deeper insights into my mother's plight, as I felt the tight binds of trauma bonding that made me feel that choking contradiction that I was with a man who took pleasure in slowly snuffing me out, like a cat playing with a half-dead mouse, whilst I still felt the heart pangs of not wanting to breathe without him. Hot, cold, in, out, I love you, I loathe you, devaluing, dismissing, rejecting, then love bombing, praising. I was the good girl and the bad girl, he would actually say that. I remembered this feeling. I've lived this before with my father. I would view myself with a critical, logical eye from outside of my body, while the pain of losing him anchored me into a freeze response. I felt weak to his love. That chemical rush I confused with love was my wound vibrating. I left whilst madly, deeply in love because I knew I had to. Over time and progressively he got worse and I saw the mask fall off.

We were in the kitchen and he was looking at me sideways, a strange smirk on his face. We were talking about getting counselling as he had previously said he wanted me to stay, but in this moment, without any provocation, he said, 'I bet you feel abandoned, don't you.' There it was, that jaw-dropping, textbook moment where the mask falls. He knew my wounds and there, with his figurative sword, he stabbed me, with the truth of what he was doing to me. They love to tell you who they are and what they plan to do to you; it's part of the game.

We never had a conversation despite my many attempts to know what exactly was happening. It just stopped, like a guillotine, with no conversations, no goodbyes, like a book that suddenly stops mid-sentence, with no end, no conclusion. It was designed for maximum hurt.

I suffered deeply from that ending, but I dusted myself off again and then I stood back up. I learned a long time ago it's not about the pain, the grief or the fear that will always be there, sometimes more than others, but we can and must always get up. I envisioned Muhammed Ali, knocked out on the boxing ring floor, blood draining out of his eyes and nose, the referee counting, 1, 2, 3, 4, 5, 6, 7, 8, 9; my pinkie starts twitching, my eyes strain to open, I drag myself across the floor until I get on one knee, then the other and stager my way back up, because I will always get back up. I will always stand UP!

There is no forever with a Cluster B, no happy ending and no it will get better. I learnt that from my mother's marriage of fifty-eight years to a Cluster B, it always will and can only get worse. They smell those childhood wounds of abandonment on even the most trained. They love the strong ones, the ones most likely to stay as, after all, it's a game and you are checkmate. I refused to lie in the same pile of all the exes, bitches, those psychos he always referred to them as. It was not a pile I would, will ever, lay down in. That's a choice!

I learned so much about myself from that relationship. The love I felt was so profound, but I realised it was the love I was projecting. It was my love mirrored back. That love was my higher self to my ten-year-old inner child.

I learned after that to seek the kind of love that is calm, consistent, supportive, stable and encouraging and to sit more with those deeper parts of me that still searched for validation in men. I learned to feed her spirit with love from other sources, self-generated and not be dependent on a man. Only then could I truly give love in return.

Later in life, I met a man who was much older than me. He was brilliant, funny and Jewish. I met him in my human sexuality class; he was my professor. I knew by the way he marked my assignments with such bold red text and 10/10 ratings he was at least intrigued. We flirted furiously, albeit subtly, as we were always viewed under the watchful eyes of my classmates. Once the course ended, we both lingered behind and ended up in the elevator alone. We didn't say a word to each other, just a glance, and as soon as the doors closed, we were embraced in a long-awaited kiss. It was worth it.

He was exciting, open, honest, incredibly intelligent and a wonderful healer on my path. I welcomed his kind of distraction and he too needed mine. We moved in together into a large house in a good area. We had a maid, a nanny for the kids and he bought me a red sports car. He was incredibly generous and loved to surprise me with gifts. Always a foodie, I loved matzo ball soup, cheese blintzes and his mother. She was the kindest woman and a stereotype of all jokes made about a Jewish mother.

I remember driving with her from Montreal to Florida, a two-day trip somewhere along the most tedious nothingness of North and South Carolina. I heard my partner say, 'Ma, you want some chocolate?'

'What do I need chocolate for, Jerry?'

'Ma, you must be hungry, have some chocolate.'

'Do I look like I need chocolate?'

'Ma, here, take the chocolate.'

'I said I don't want any chocolate.'

'OK, Ma, OK.'

Two minutes later, after we ate the chocolate, she said, 'What, I can't have any chocolate? I could die in the back here before anybody offers me anything.'

He proposed to me several times, but I always hesitated. I wasn't ready, I'd say. We were together for several years, but our relationship was never destined to be forever. I knew that then. Our age gap of sixteen years then was fine, but each decade the gap would escalate and widen our differences in everything. An older friend of his took me aside and warned me of that. I heeded his advice. He was a very important man on my journey in life, as his wisdom, humour and adoration toward me re-enacted that male role model I needed to feel, experience and trust. He was a significant man on that road of my life. In the end, he wanted me to convert to Judaism, it became an ultimatum. As much as I find all beliefs fascinating, my culture of Celtic, Norse and old ways runs through my blood and heart and I could not grant him that wish.

I call myself a serial monogamous, as I've had long-term relationships that endured but ended. My quest for forever was strained under the intolerance of my standards to stay safe. I believe in growth over longevity. To have both, however, is ideal.

I loved living in Montreal. It was and is a magical place.It's the people that make it special. There is a consciousness within them that far surpasses anywhere I've ever travelled.

They excel in an awareness of humanity and nature, a passion for culture, music and the arts and an ability to connect to others with ease. I had friends that fed my soul and was connected to various groups that shared interests in comparative religion, spirituality, paganism, psychodrama, jazz music, dance and anything that created healing. The French influence romanticised the experiences, as I'd sip on café au lait, eat pâté with a freshly baked French baguette and ice skate in winter on the canal.

My children and I shared beautiful homes and their upbringing was filled with influences that shaped their layered, cultured, expansive and deep-thinking minds. I am most proud of that and them. My life there was deeply fulfilling as I spent many decades travelling, laughing, growing, learning, experiencing and creating thousands of memories with my children that fulfilled every hope and dream I ever wanted or needed. That family I was always seeking was and is in them.

Something was shifting in Montreal. I felt it. Notorious for its political language issues causing conflicts between French-speaking and English-speaking Canadians, the divide was getting wider. Although I speak conversational Spanish and French, my language skills are from memorising phrases; I don't have that part in my brain that allows me to retain languages fully. I was, therefore, worried about my future, financially and from a career perspective. I also worried about my children's future. One spoke French, the other one only modestly. The language requirements were changing so much that one had to be fully fluent in French, both written and spoken, even to work at McDonald's. Mastering the complexities and flow needed as a therapist was a very unlikely possibility. So, when the opportunity to go to Australia arose, I took it. I always try to be ahead of the storm and Montreal was destined to experience a big one.

Chapter Twelve
The Second Wave

Moving to Australia in 2006 was a leap of faith that could only have happened because of Michael's death. It taught me that life could change in an instant and one needed to learn to listen to those opportunities, even when that change seems scary. Once you've experienced the shadow side of life; death, abuse and betrayal, you learn to see the signs of the light, trying to balance things. Ying and yang, dark and light, life wants you well. I saw it as my destiny; it was a feeling I chose over my mind that was wondering what the hell I was doing. Seize the day, carpe diem, I chose to jump.

I learned a lot during the first years of migration about the meaning of home for myself and my children. Home isn't just a house you live in; it grounds you, makes you feel safe, connected and loved and is what you identify with. Home is a subjective concept, however, and so my children each had their own experience of what that was for them. My destiny created a shift in theirs and it wasn't all positive for them. No matter how hard you try or what you think you know, mistakes can be made and our intentions to create the best course in life are all we can do.

As a migrant, that's the hardest thing about changing your homeland. All those innocuous things like your favourite restaurant, known shortcuts, bumping into old friends, old lovers, old colleagues and familiar places are gone. Those obvious associations that make us feel a part of something are reset to a clean slate. It's unnerving and takes years to replenish. Some of it is lost forever.

Even with such a big move, I was still connected to my family. Over the years, I talked to my siblings and parents most days by phone or email but stayed away from seeing them in person. It was a hard decision, but one I knew was the only way I'd survive. I needed to keep them at a healthy distance, out of my physical environment, in order to allow myself to bathe in new energy that healed, lifted, elevated and encouraged me.

There was a mix of conflicting triggers, mine and theirs, that negatively created confusion and chaos when we were together in person. Subtle innuendos, slight backhanded distinctions, micro facial expressions, throat clearing, nose sniffling, tics and even the energy or the intention brought to the space by a victim of trauma is the language so easily seen, heard and felt. To most, these layers would sound, look or feel innocuous, but to the hypersensitive, hyper-aware child of trauma, it's their first language. I had to create tight boundaries because even though we were in the abuse together, we didn't share the same experiences or perspectives. We sat in that chaos at different times, different ages, with different contexts and in different countries. We are all an island when it comes to facing our own inner world. Life is intrinsic, after all; therefore, one can only rescue themselves.

At first, I saw my parents every eight years; then, it grew to once every fifteen years. My sister Heidi and I would see each other in person once a year and she lives close to me now, although we keep a mutually healthy space. Keily and I went from seeing each other daily, living together and raising our children in the same city, to not seeing each other in person for over thirty years. Chris and I also began our earlier years always catching up in The Bahamas or Vancouver, but we then stayed away from each other for over thirty years, except for one last visit a few years before his death.

Staying away was the hardest thing I had to do, but it was necessary for survival. I know I would not be alive today had I continued seeing them. The re-experiencing of that toxic chaos that we were collectively associated with would have killed me; in many ways, it almost did.

Those emails over the years are in the thousands; I have them all sitting in my inbox. A few decades of conversations, confessions, truths, pains, loves and laughter shared has taken its own form in a family book. I cherish it because it represents my role for decades as the mediator, the one everyone turned to behind the scenes; I was the neutral, safe territory. They knew I cared. I understood and loved them all deeply. They needed that; I needed that too.

The power of staying away allowed us to write behind the veil of protection, just our words expressed; it was healing, connecting and held us all into feeling we had a family and were OK. Beyond the chaos and wounds of our family are people filled with deep, layered, creative, intelligent, wonderful and purposeful talents. I'm proud of my family, the roots we were birthed from run deep into the richness of the earth; at least we didn't completely miss out on that. Through those emails, I unconsciously created a forum where we all had a voice to share and connect; it was our safe place, our home away from home.

I wrote to my parents and siblings most days, sharing wonderful updates about the crazy birds in Australia that woke me up at the earliest hours of the morning, the long car rides everywhere and how the weather changed several times a day. I sent pictures of my travels to Alice Springs, Queensland, climbing the Sydney Harbour Bridge and standing out on the rocks at Bushranger's Bay, where natural crystals form on the cliff's edge. Our emails were mostly happy and positive, about travel, art, music, adventures, new love, children and grandchildren and we were able to keep them in the present of what we were living, creating and loving. Those emails were mutually healing for all of us and highlighted a phrase I coined about reinventing the life we need to support our path forward in our healing. Regardless of the past, all children need to feel some connection to their parents, as they are a part of them. With trauma, that becomes very difficult and the brain can only take so much chaos at once, so much loss. If we don't chunk it down into more malleable bite sizes, we will choke on its overwhelming force.

So, my emails allowed me to believe and visualise a more loving and healthier family, a family that was more 'well', with interpersonal connections that felt deeper and more real than perhaps they were. I coined it 'Conscious Illusion'.

As I had been studying Buddhism for some time, I was always challenging myself to wake up, challenge my concepts of reality and face illusions or delusions. However, that creates its own confrontation that can over-accelerate the existential climb to self-realisation. Conscious Illusion was my reconciliation of noting I was consciously aware, as I chose to be in illusion. That meant I could control it, knew I was doing it, but allowed the unreality, the fantasy of a well-connected, happier and healthier family, so I could continue to feel safe whilst I worked on myself. It's a term I often gift my clients. The brain must be given the time it needs to re-encode such layered and complex injuries. It can heal but only with space, time and the right environment.

I received an email from my father, however, that had a funny, shocking and surreal tone to it, as he talked about a movie that was filmed in our old home on Queens, in West Vancouver. It had been filmed years earlier, but he had only just gotten a VHS copy of it. *Assault and Matrimony* is a film from the late eighties about a man and wife who were constantly trying to kill each other. Accusing each other of affairs, the husband wants to move to the Caribbean; the wife wants him dead. Their fights are dangerous and yet contradicted by their formal dinners, curt conversations and feigned civility whilst seated at a long table in their dining room. Keeping up appearances amid total insanity and chaos seems to hold their stance on maintaining a standard. They even have an Old English Sheepdog; well-groomed and fun-loving, it frolics through their perfectly manicured lawn, creating a distraction for the neighbours of a successful life in the burbs.

The parallels to my parents' story were uncannily detailed and accurate. I wondered if either of the two men that bought the house on Queens worked as a screenwriter or producer or knew the person who was. Someone must have known the story of my parents' relationship; if not, it's an eerie coincidence. After viewing it themselves, my parents laughed at how accurate it was but joked it made them look much better than they really were.

Father said, 'The truth is, we were much worse'. He laughed at how hilarious that was. It's a shocking statement if you watch the movie.

Australia finally became home after several years. I learnt that after going back to Montreal a few years later to get the things I'd left in storage. I had observed myself while in Australia, unwittingly saying to all my newly acquired friends in an exaggerated accent to highlight being a foreigner, 'In my country, the coffee is better.' 'In my country, the people bring you into their homes and you can become friends, just like that.' 'In my country, restaurants are much cheaper and the food is better.' Then within the first week of going back to Canada, I heard myself repeating the same sentences, but now I was referencing Australia. 'In Australia, the coffee is so much better.' 'In Australia, you can eat at the best restaurants.' After that, I knew Australia had become my true home.

My career was thriving, my life felt balanced and inspired and those childhood years were far behind me; I barely even thought of them. I would run most days, ten-to-fifteen kilometres, hike, lift weights and cycle—I loved feeling strong. Everything in my life, all I had worked for in myself, succeeded. I was happy. It was that kind of happiness that answered my hypothesis of why some people make it beyond their childhood traumas and others don't. Consistency, hard work, a lot of therapy, physical fitness, nature, a life that pushes you toward change and new experiences, symbols, self-awareness, hope, love, curiosity, philosophy and a spiritual purpose—and most importantly, always, family. My life had meaning, direction and I was proud of who I was and what I chose to do with what I got. I had to take that path that left my body scarred from its thorns, but I kept climbing and running toward that goal. I hypothesised all those years ago that I could do it, despite what psychology said and here I was; the view was so much better at the top.

While my life was thriving, my siblings also sought ways to ease the symptoms of their past and create a life worth living. Heidi was always expressing herself through her art and pushing herself to believe more in its value and in her own. She entered art shows, took courses, created greeting cards and sold her work in galleries, privately and at local shops. She even followed me to Australia, where she travelled solo, experiencing life on a cattle station and wonderful small towns across the desert.

Keily was writing, travelling, dating and exploring spiritual and religious belief systems, looking for meaning and ways to further heal. She was also passionate about plant-based foods and still carried a deep and inseparable bond with dogs. She was reconnecting deep bonds with her children and was the happiest I've ever heard her with the news of her grandchildren; they gave her so much joy. Chris pursued his music, travel, Buddhism and many other inspired learnings as he had many talents. He found solace in Buddhism after almost dying of a widow maker heart attack and, at least for a few years, it seemed to calm his mind.

There was an episode, however, in Mexico. My father sent me an email telling me about it in detail. He said he had 'washed his hands' of Chris. He described a story in which Chris arrived for a visit but seemed very angry. Chris was telling my parents he knew who they really were—witches. He accused Father of wasting all his inheritance on his own selfish interests and Mother of being spineless and co-dependent. He told Father he 'spat in the face of him' and motioned to spit. Father was enraged. Chris left in the

very early hours the next morning; Mother ran after him and fell
to the ground, crying in complete despair. Father said he would
never forgive him for that and he never did. That ended their
already very fractured relationship. Chris, clearly under the throws
of psychosis, ended up in a psych ward for a time. His diagnosis
wasn't definitive, but in an email he said, 'I have a kind of crazy
that becomes obsessed with power, control and revenge.'

There is a very fine line between absolute brilliance and
madness and at times, Chris stood on that fragile precipice. It was
the dark side of him I'd seen, bubbling up at different times in my
life, no doubt stirred from its slumber from a concoction of drugs,
alcohol and a long time battling the lack of reconciliation in so
many areas of his life under the reign of Father.

Years went by and although I communicated with everyone
through email, no one was speaking with anyone else. Things were
getting too hard to navigate and trust as some of my siblings were
changing course. Unresolved traumas were facing the turbulent
waters of all those years of repressed tears, like a loose thread
hanging precariously off a jumper, one tug risked unravelling it all.
Things were about to get worse.

Mother and Father were seemingly well. No doubt, behind
the scenes, the drunken violence continued, but I was only getting
updated on the good bits. They were travelling every six months
between their homes in Canada and Mexico. Mother seemed
happy; she was winning awards for her paintings and playing
competitive tennis, even at her age. Father talked a lot about his
eyesight as it was deteriorating progressively. He also struggled
with gut health issues from a bug he suspected he picked up in
Mexico. They were trying every health trick— aloe vera juice,

rooibos tea, Metamucil. I'd get weekly updates with the details of their much-improved bowel movements. I always found it funny they'd drink aloe vera juice and make all these efforts whilst smoking copious amounts of cigarettes and drinking alcohol. There isn't a photo to be found of my parents without an ashtray, a cigarette, a crystal tumbler or a raised glass; cheers was their go-to for photos. At least, for now, they sounded happier.

Father sent an urgent email that said Keily was diagnosed with stage two breast cancer. The news hit me so hard that I fell to the kitchen floor. Not Keily, it's not fair, I thought. She had endured unimaginable trauma not just the shared trauma of our childhoods but ongoing trauma, as she just never managed to grab onto any of the lifelines. Her wounds festered as she suffered in her own ruminations, deep anger and confusion over all those things that could never be reconciled. She felt the physical and emotional pains from the domino effects of her embittered sufferings that eventually bled into the lives of her children. The cycle of our generational inherited abuse continued. Kind, funny and intelligent, she was always feeling stuck, held down by the one question she asked me on so many occasions—why? Why had our entire lives been about so much suffering? Why did the parents she loved leave her with so much pain? Why? She bathed in its toxic, insatiable quest that no one could answer until it drowned her.

The theory of randomness is the only answer I discovered, as our minds create delusions and expectations that can lead us to some of our greatest confusions. It is the belief or expectation that if we are good or nice to others, we will receive the same in turn. The truth, however, is bad things can happen to good people. At times, life is just a game of Russian roulette. It isn't personal, although it feels like it is. In all its joy and trauma, it's just a series of random and unfortunate events. Some people get far more than they need or deserve. There is no silver lining or beautiful epiphany in all things. Life can be cruel, unfair, unjust, shit, catastrophic and you didn't deserve any of those things that face-planted you and shredded a part of your mind and body with everlasting wounds. I am so sorry you suffered. I am so sorry you endured any of those things that harmed you. You didn't deserve it. I believe you, I hear you, I witness you and I stand here with you. It happened, but you can find a way forward that can elevate you back to a place where you can reclaim your mind, your body, your dignity, and your right to narrate the story you chose for yourself. With your own gilded gold pen in hand, you have the right to stand up and the power to rewrite wellness, purpose, hope, healing, grace, gratitude, unforgiving, power and victory into YOU.

I wish so deeply Keily could have found that pen and those words for herself. She suffered through surgeries, pain and ill health for several years. Her cancer progressed from stage two to stage four within the first few months, so her time became focused on living her life from a perspective of quality over quantity. She tried to find beauty through the cracks.

It was only a year later when I received an email from Chris telling me he had been diagnosed with stage four metastatic prostate cancer and that it was in his bones. He discovered it after going to a massage therapist with severe back pain. Feeling worse after the massage, he went to the doctor and discovered a tumour that had fractured his lumbar 4. I was devastated.

My two siblings, who over the years embodied so much of the trauma of our childhoods, continued to ingest even more through their many shared visits with our parents over the years. In their own quest to seek answers, they didn't stay away. I knew the word cancer was just the physical manifestation of what their minds and body endured. The rage, the pain and the confusion of their entire lives of chronic, endless trauma turned to a poison they swallowed so deeply that it metastasised. My two siblings, who deserved to be gifted with an extension of life, were instead having it ripped away from them.

Life is out of our control and it certainly isn't fair. We all sit precariously on that edge; we just don't know how fragile we really are. It's why our moments count more than our time. Life is a currency we must spend wisely.

Mother called me out of the blue; she never called, she wasn't allowed to, but I recognised her voice immediately. 'Dad's getting worse,' she said and hung up. I called so many times after that, but she couldn't say anything as he was always around. I planned to visit, even organising the dates with Father and buying the tickets to fly to Mexico, but Father would uninvite me. That wasn't unusual, it was a sport to him, but I was worried about my mother and that call.

I received an email from Father in 2013. 'Mum is in hospital, she has metastasised lung cancer and she needs you to come.' I flew to Mexico immediately, flying first to LA and then on a small prop plane with Alaska Airlines to Guadalajara. Once at the airport, I was instructed to only take a registered taxi as the cartel was reactivated and rampant in that area. I arrived at the hotel twenty-nine hours later, exhausted, hungry and emotionally spent. I was concerned about seeing my father after all these years. I had the trust and confidence in myself; however, having been a therapist

for years and feeling competent and strong in my sense of self, I
had the tools to manage whatever he threw my way. Besides, his
wife was dying, I thought. I'm here to support my mother and he
invited me, surely now things will be OK.

I scanned the lobby of the hotel on arrival but couldn't see
him. Then I heard his voice, 'Deirdre, you're here.' My heart
sank; in front of me was this old man, average height, completely
grey, his eyelids drooped, his breathing short and heavy, dressed
immaculately in a tweed jacket, polished leather shoes with tubes
running out of his nose that connected to an oxygen tank beside
him. He was my father. I was shocked as I realised my memory of
him was outdated; he seemed fragile.

Father invited me to join him for a drink; I could see he was
still trying to hold on to the stoic man we all knew or he wanted
us to know him to be. He told me Mother was in her last hours; in
fact, it was unlikely she would make it through the night.

Valentia, his granddaughter, my niece, was at the hospital with
her. Mum was in a coma, but Valentia told her I was coming. I
wanted so much to see my mother immediately, but it was unsafe
to travel at night, so I went to the hotel room Valentia had been
staying in for weeks. I hadn't known until then Mother had been
unwell for weeks.

I woke up after five hours, dressed in a nice white shirt, a
black leather skirt that covered my knees and low-heeled pumps.
I wanted to look my best for Mother. Father was staying in the
adjoining room, so before I left for the hospital, I popped in to
say good morning and check in on him. His first sentence, after
scanning me up and down with his eyes disapprovingly, was,

'You do realise you look like a prostitute, don't you?' I was aghast; after all this time, this was still happening.

'I know Mexico well, this is appropriate and elegant and I'm happy with how I look. And I don't look like a prostitute.'

I arrived at the entrance of the hospital and saw Valentia waiting at the front to greet me. She had the most welcoming and warmest smile; it reassured me and gave me my second wind. She was a breath of fresh air. She immediately hugged me and prepared me for what my mother looked like; at least she tried her best to. As I stood at the end of her bed in the ICU, Mother looked emaciated. Less than fifty kilograms, she had thin, white hair, deep wrinkles and her skin was grey; in fact, she looked dead. No one could live in that condition, I thought, except my mother. I said, 'Hi Mum, I love you. I'm here.'

I hadn't seen my mother since I was thirty-six years old. I was now forty-nine. Within seconds her head moved, her eyes pried open and she said, 'Deirdre, is that you?' I heard Valentia gasp and the nurse suddenly rushed out. She came back with the attending doctors and other nurses on the ward, several of whom were doing the sign of the cross on their chest.

'It's incredible,' the doctor said. 'I don't believe it; she was not meant to live.'

I was holding Mother's hand, telling her I loved her, reassuring her I was there. She kept asking, 'Deirdre, is that you? Is it really you?'

'Yes, it's really me, Mum.'

It was a powerful moment. All our years apart did nothing to sever our unique and powerful bond. Father tried very hard to sabotage that connection, keeping us apart as much as he could. He knew how close and sacred our bond was, so to keep us apart was the perfect punishment. The goal was to strip me of my mother and to strip my mother of the opportunity for a family. Divide and conquer, as no one was allowed to form any true alliances. Father forgot one thing; Mother and I spoke several languages that weren't dependent on time or space. The language of symbols, the language of the intuitive, the language of energy and the language of love. We communicated all the time in our dreams, in our minds, in our hearts and in our souls. Every minute I stood there, the cumulation of our shared love caused her to bounce back with a new vibrancy, so much so she was transferred back into general care within a few hours.

I spent nine weeks, every day, with my mother. I did the day shifts and Valentia often took the night shifts. We talked about everything, her childhood memories, stories about her boyfriends, her studies, Father, her mother and guardians, her paintings, her truth and her confessions. I took notes as she shared all the stories, filling in the blanks for things she left out over all those years. She joked she was the fly on the wall and grinned as she said it. She wanted her story heard. She told me she wanted her story told. She made me promise I would write this book for her, for our family and for me. I promised.

Mother was much more aware of every detail about her family. She was lucid and had a sharp mind with an astute psychotherapeutic viewpoint and she didn't miss a beat. There were parts of her children she didn't like and she told me, but she always ended those stories with, 'I loved all my children.'

She was raw, honest and candid and said she knew she was a martyr but couldn't leave our father. She said no matter what she tried and how much I tried to save her, she would never have left. She asked me so many questions about my life, my choices, my thoughts and my childhood and then asked me what my favourite memory was.

'Picking shells on the beach with you, Mum,' I said.

Her eyes welled with tears and I could see she was taken aback. She didn't think she deserved to be so loved and valued like that, but she did; she deserved a lifetime of love. She was my beautiful mother.

She'd been an avid painter for years, mostly watercolours, so I asked her, 'What's your favourite painting you ever did?'

'The one I haven't painted yet?' she said.

'What's that one about.'

'You and I are picking shells on the beach.'

My mother finally told me she loved me in the best way she could.

A priest walked down the hallway past my mother's hospital room. A dedicated pagan, she should have sent him on; instead, she waved him in. She wanted to share in the wine and bread, she said. Her frail, bony, pale white hands reached out for that chalice of wine and held it straight back as she drank every drop down. It wasn't her finest moment. She was in a forced sobriety and wine was too tempting to pass by. We laughed so joyously at how silly and naughty that was.

Toward the end of my stay, Mother asked me when my scheduled departure date was. I blurted it out, but mid-sentence I realised by the way she was looking at me that she was going to die before I left. I tried to retract my words. I promised I could change the date, but it was already done. Only a week before I was scheduled to leave, Mother started the dying process. It began with her slipping in and out of consciousness, saying odd things like, 'I'm riding my pink bicycle to Australia' or telling me she couldn't believe how tall my son was now or how beautiful my daughter had become or how much she loved seeing the other children and grandchildren.

Twenty-four hours later, I sat on her bed. Valentia was next to me, holding my hand in support as we watched her oxygenator attached to her ring finger. Measuring her oxygen levels was like celebrating New Year's Eve backward. The countdown to death began, 92, 86, 80, 76, 74, 60, 58, 55, 47, 42. By the time we got to the countdown, she was catatonic, seemingly unaware until the last number. Then she starkly opened her eyes and said, 'Don't be angry, it killed my family.' Her eyes wide open, she said it loudly and sharply and pointed her finger to highlight how important that message was and then she exhaled one final breath. I remember thinking, 'Why did she say that I'm not angry? What did she mean?' I knew it would reveal itself one day.

Her death was not a struggle; in fact, she left with beauty, grace and trust in her belief in a life after death and a cycle of reincarnation. Despite my father's request they both be buried side by side, Mother secretly said to me, 'Why would I want to spend my afterlife with him, wasn't this one lifetime enough?' We had a good giggle at that.

I was sitting at the long oak table in my father's Mexican home when her ashes arrived. Father didn't understand my reaction to his comments, as grief to him wasn't something you spent much time on. I didn't want to stay at his house after

Mother died. Father hadn't been terribly pleasant behind the scenes during those weeks I was with her on her deathbed.

My mind was spinning as my father's projections created a world of unreality that was an unsafe place for me to grieve. I refused to expose my mind or my body to his deviant ideas and his unquenchable thirst to exercise what he deemed his power. It was of no value to me as I held my own vulnerability tightly bound to my mother, whose death was still filling my mind with the images and sounds of love. I left for the sacredness of us as we both deserved that space to honour all we were to each other. I buried my mother's ashes under the apple tree in my garden once home in Australia. I placed a pink bicycle in front of it, just as she had imagined before she died. I know she would have loved that.

Six months later, I was flying to see my brother, whom I hadn't seen in thirty years. He was in palliative care and was using his uncertain time left in life to travel, so he rented a place in Florence, Italy. I had to go; I needed to see my brother at least one more time, for me. He greeted me at the train station in Rome. He looked the same, albeit older, as we both were, but he was my beautiful brother. I felt elated. Our time together was powerful bonding and I felt the closeness we shared from when I was much younger. The warnings my parents were regularly sending me emails about over the previous years, about his mental health, his darker side and not being the same brother, didn't matter. I remember thinking it wasn't fair to judge him on those things, as I knew the amazing brother he was before trauma took over. I needed to prove it to myself. I wanted to see and believe only the good side, perhaps I even needed it.

There were two things Chris said at that time that caused me to flinch and take note. The first was said in front of his wife and my then-partner. He said, 'I don't find you even the least bit attractive anymore.'

Huh? A pin could have dropped in the room as we all felt lost in its oddity. The second thing he said was, 'Don't need or want any of Father's inheritance. Walk away.' It felt manipulative.

I was only back home in Australia a week when the phone rang; it was Armando letting me know Father wasn't well and I needed to fly back to Mexico. It was Christmas and flights weren't easy to get, but I flew to New Zealand, then San Francisco, then Guadalajara. I was back in Mexico, this time to sit bedside with my father.

When I arrived at his home, I was shocked to find him in diapers. There were so many people coming and going. Something felt off. I saw no signs of his iPad or phone and struggled to get any signal when I used my own phone. Armando said they had been having trouble with the Wi-Fi. He said he would call the local company to come and fix the problem, but no one came. The overseeing doctor was driving Father's car; apparently, he had given it to her. Armando was driving my mother's car and he was turning up to work drunk. The state of the house was not how my father liked; known to be OCD, he kept a tight, immaculate ship. The house had broken locks on the windows, the kitchen was dirty, the couch had ripped and something felt off.

Father, bedridden, I now learned for over two months, was unaware of all the people coming in and out as he was stuck in his suite in the back part of the house. He couldn't believe I had come. We had an argument months before when he called me one day completely unexpectedly.

'Do you think you're clever, do you? You're not. You're not intelligent, you know that, don't you? You think you're somebody being a therapist, but you're nobody, do you hear me? Nobody, nothing. You're a fucking idiot, do you know that. Do you know you're a fucking idiot?'

I had no idea what prompted his unprovoked attack. I held that phone to my ear and froze, my body shaking, tears seeping out of my eyes; he caught me completely off guard. I was trembling. I had no idea why he did that. Something must have happened. Someone must have said something to make him angry, I thought.

It wasn't until I was there in Mexico that he told me he was angry at me because he didn't trust our brother and thought I was aligned with him to challenge the will. Heidi had mentioned to him that I went to visit Chris in Italy. He had warned me not to go back then, but I went anyways, as it just didn't make sense. He said Chris wasn't the same person anymore.

'Maybe it was caused by the drugs he did when he was younger, I don't know,' he said.

I told my father that I had visited Chris because I loved him and that I did not think he would ever do anything to harm him. I just assumed my father was being the usual sceptic and antagonist he often was.

Upon seeing me there by his bedside, however, he reached out for my hand and told me he was happy I was there. 'Stay close, kid,' he said. 'I need you.' I had never heard my father say that before. I never saw him vulnerable. I felt so much love for him at that moment. I still needed that. I was happy to be there; in fact, it was a compelling urge I had to be there. I couldn't let my father die alone, in diapers, with no one there to support him, regardless of what he did. He was my father. Besides, it said more about who I was, I thought.

My father was dying. He was scared. He was worried about what he had done in his life; no doubt he had many more secrets I didn't know. He asked one of the attending nurses to comb his hair, bathe him and get him ready for his deceased wife; he was ready to see her for Christmas. As I sat next to him, holding his hand and stroking his hair, it was both an honour and a very difficult feeling, as this was the man who poisoned my two siblings with cancer. I wanted to set things right for all of us, so I said, 'Dad, we all forgive you.' To which he looked at me perplexed and said, 'I forgive you,' and there it was: the truth I never wanted to see. Always hoping for more, expecting more, he showed up consistently, even in this dying moment, he was exactly who he'd always been; he flipped the script. 'I forgive you,' he said.

Huh? What? 'All these years of abuse, you forgive us?' I laughed out loud. It was funny. Not that moment but the bigger picture. I was laughing at myself. At that moment, he erased so many years of suffering because I realised so much of it was wanting, hoping and striving for more. Yes, he was a psychopath. He never hid it; we just didn't want to accept it. With that, he choked, sputtered and died in the same way he lived life, with resistance and aggression, fighting against it all. My father, always one to ensure he left an everlasting impression on our minds, died on Christmas Day. How could any one of us ever forget that?

I didn't want to tell my siblings their father died on Christmas; they deserved to have that day for themselves. I waited until

Boxing Day to call. However, I had noticed in hindsight that not one of them called him. It was an observation I reflected on in the years to come.

The phone calls to my siblings were hard to deliver. My sisters took the news with grace that the end of the king that reigned had so many conflicting emotions. It was the call to my brother, however, that set the tone for the next ten years of my life. The worst ten years I'd ever endured, the second wave.

I called in the evening, his time. Chris had been drinking and our conversation lasted three-and-a-half hours. Several times, I heard his wife intercept the conversation, trying to get him to go to bed, but he insisted on talking. It started with the word solidarity; he had spoken of it when we were in Italy. I understood it to mean we would stand together to honour Father's wishes, to ensure things were done according to his will, protecting the family name with honour. It wasn't what Chris meant. He said solidarity was toward him, that we were the intelligent ones and together we could stall our sisters into accepting whatever meagre payout we gave them. He even told me about the division of this new inheritance. Fifty thousand for each of the girls, sixty per cent for himself and forty per cent would be left for me. Considering the estate was anticipated to be in the millions, our sisters weren't being treated very fairly.

I immediately said no. He called me a fucking idiot then warned me, 'You know, Deirdre, in Mexico, one could easily hire someone for five thousand dollars to do whatever they want for them. Tread lightly. I'd hate to think you end up in a Mexican prison or, worse, dead.' I froze, chills rushed through my body as I looked at Valentia and my partner sitting next to me, mouthing the words in a panicked whisper, telling them what was happening, feeling a desperate sense of needing to be witnessed. I knew it was a serious and very real threat. I did what I have always done; I immediately voiced every detail to my partner and niece as if they were taking a statement. I sent emails to my sisters, panicked, telling them about that conversation and how scared I was. I wrote to our family lawyer. I wanted it documented. They all did what I suppose anyone would have done, they minimised it. 'Oh, he was probably just drunk', 'He didn't mean it, he is just trying to scare you.' I was scared. Father was right. Chris wasn't the same.

Father made me an agent to the executor. It means very little, except that I had the responsibility of assisting the lawyers and being on the front lines of what became an estate war, taking hits without any armour. It's a very dangerous position to be in after all those years, with two siblings dying from the unresolved pain of their childhood trauma. Father dead, no longer any other outlet to reconcile all that rage, that fury, I was the sacrificial lamb.

Father's seemingly innocent act of making me an agent, simply because I was the mediator, became Father chose her as the favourite. It was too much for them to bear. I braced myself for the conflict I had in myself, of standing strong in the trenches as the final wish of my father and to the values and duty I hold so strongly, yet not wanting to be used as a pawn for his final act. It felt like this was his last play in that game of chess. The black ants and the red ants. He often warned us he would set us up at the end to battle, then he'd laugh, as we would too, to what we thought was a sarcastic joke. It seems now it wasn't.

It was another ten years before the family estate was settled. Enormous amounts of money were lost, largely spent on lawyers.

The battle fought against our brother who delayed, intercepted, accused and sent numerous emails attacking everything about the estate, including personal attacks about my weight, my career, my choice of studies, to anything that would wound, devalue, denounce, belittle and create pain in those old wounds. He wanted to rip them wide open and tear me down—it worked. Those hits were worse than the first rounds of childhood, as what had sustained me for all those years was knowing at least I had my siblings. I loved them so dearly.

Like Father, the real focus got lost and those dark triads of rage, jealousy and revenge took over my brother. Death stirs the bottom of the pot. Life became full circle and the wounds turned wild, like monkeys in a zoo, the zookeeper gone, they were out of their cages and throwing their shit everywhere.

During those ten years, Keily died in 2020 and Chris died six months later, in 2021. They died fighting, under stress and with so many things unresolved for them. There is no win in that. I cried for my siblings and tried to mourn their passing, but my body, by this time, was still enduring a newly reactivated diagnosis of PTSD. It had been building; how could it not? None of us was immune. Daily and multiple emails sent over the years, an ending of a relationship, my siblings dying six months apart, the machine gun firing of chaos, it was inevitably going to shoot me down. An irony to my life of trying to out-chase guns.

I had moved to the country and was in the beginning stages of building my new home. I was standing by my car in the small town minutes from my home when suddenly I couldn't move or talk. I was frozen. It was incredibly scary for someone who has studied the mind for so many years, my body had had enough. It was a while before I could move well enough to get my phone and call my daughter. A therapist herself, she coached me back to my car and assisted me in calling my therapist. I'd been seeing him throughout the entire decade of battling the family estate. How could I ensure I was safe and effective to work with my own clients if I didn't trust and believe in the same system I stood for? He helped me enormously at that moment, formally diagnosing me on the spot. I took a break and flew on my own to Bali for five weeks. I ran daily, meditated, walked, ate clean and reset, reclaimed, mourned and revived myself. Like the Tarahumara tribe I read about in the book *Born to Run*, I ran from a place of pure joy until I could feel it, living back inside my body once more.

I have an altar at home with pictures of my two siblings from a time in our childhood when we all trusted the love we had for each other. It was a time in those windows between the chaos of trauma we endured. Building forts in the forest, swimming with the otters, building snowmen, drinking endless cups of tea while Chris played the guitar and sang, Keily applied my make-up and I baked cookies or granola bars from scratch. We philosophised about everything in life and fed our minds and hearts on the binds of our shared stories.

We often said we loved each other, told the others they were beautiful or handsome, listened with respect for the incredible intelligence and creative minds we expressed; we honoured each other as the antidote to all that ailed us. Back then, we were a strong force to be reckoned with. That's how I choose to remember my siblings—for their bravery, unconditional love, kindness and incredibly powerful, unique and layered minds.

They existed and they were so much more than the fragments left behind at their passing.

Keily chose to have a white butterfly on her urn. There are many days during the warmer months when I see a white butterfly pause to rest by my feet or flutter around me to grab my attention. I always say, 'Hi Keily' when I see her. Chris is always in the sound of guitars or in the generation of grandchildren who illustrate his same musical genius. I imagine sometimes he is whispering in their ears, co-creating, inspiring some of their music now. My mother, who always drew the monarch butterfly, flutters furiously around my head so often I am forced to stop and acknowledge her. I always do so with a feeling of incredible love and a sense of laughter at how insistent she can be. My father, the part of the man I choose to remember, leaves me with the poem *Desiderata*, his favourite or at least it was a prominent feature in our home.

Desiderata

Go placidly amid the noise and the haste,
and remember what peace there may be in silence.
As far as possible, without surrender,
be on good terms with all persons.
Speak your truth quietly and clearly;
and listen to others,
even to the dull and the ignorant;
they too have their story.
Avoid loud and aggressive persons;
they are vexatious to the spirit.
If you compare yourself with others,

you may become vain or bitter,

for always there will be greater and lesser persons than yourself.

Enjoy your achievements as well as your plans.

Keep interested in your own career, however humble;

it is a real possession in the changing fortunes of time.

Exercise caution in your business affairs,

for the world is full of trickery.

But let this not blind you to what virtue there is;

many persons strive for high ideals,

and everywhere life is full of heroism.

Be yourself. Especially do not feign affection.

Neither be cynical about love,

for in the face of all aridity and disenchantment,

it is as perennial as the grass.

Take kindly the counsel of the years,

gracefully surrendering the things of youth.

Nurture strength of spirit to shield you in sudden misfortune.

But do not distress yourself with dark imaginings.

Many fears are born of fatigue and loneliness.

Beyond a wholesome discipline,

be gentle with yourself.

You are a child of the universe

no less than the trees and the stars;

you have a right to be here.

And whether or not it is clear to you,

no doubt the universe is unfolding as it should.

Therefore, be at peace with God,

whatever you conceive Him to be.

And whatever your labors and aspirations,

in the noisy confusion of life,

keep peace in your soul.

With all its sham, drudgery, and broken dreams,

it is still a beautiful world.

Be cheerful. Strive to be happy.

       — Max Ehrmann (1872–1945), written in 1927

Not everything in life is all good or all bad, just as we are not one whole but a series of multiple parts. Therefore, we can choose to negotiate the ratio of what parts or what percentage we want to keep and what parts we discard or fade. For my mother, I keep eighty per cent; the other twenty—the drunken car rides, the inability to leave, the martyr and submission—I let fade while I hold on to her incredible grit, deep intuitive and trained psychological wisdom, her humour, her laughter and the way she smelt in her mustard-coloured jumper like my loving, beautiful Mum.

I have used this formula to negotiate the parts I chose to remember, to savour and hold onto and the parts I let go of with all my family members, just as I have done so within myself on the journey toward becoming me. The me I wanted to be, without losing my story but by rewriting it into something softer, healthier and stronger. I took my figurative pen, gold, gilded with a crown resting on the top and I re-narrated myself to transcend from the victim into the victor.

The word victor came to me in reading about Winston Churchill. During World War II, he was often photographed with his hand raised and his palm facing toward the camera with two fingers forming a 'V'. It stood for the word victor, which meant victory and 'I have overcome'. What I especially loved about it was at times he would be corrected for what seemed like an error and the photographer noted his hand was palm side facing in—therefore the 'V' would mean 'up yours' to some. 'Oh no,' he'd say, 'that is correct. I want them to know I'm saying "up yours".'

I love his humour, his strength and his guts to own his right not to forgive or accept atrocities that are too unconscionable to his values and psyche. He stood up.

Chapter Thirteen
The Act of Unforgiving

When people say, 'The past is the past, it's over', they don't understand that trauma isn't gone, it's dormant. The volcanic tremors threaten to explode with lethal, catastrophic consequences ready to engulf you at any time. We think it's never going to happen until it does. So, the past, in many cases, is still a very real threat to a survivor's existence.

The past happened, so how does one un-fuck themselves from the rape that has so intruded on their being? How does one un-destroy, un-abandon, un-annihilate, un-devalue, un-denounce themselves? To believe you can't rid yourself of the never-ending burdens swallowed into your body, inhaled into your spirit and absorbed into your mind becomes its own torture, the greatest of which I discovered was 'lack of reconciliation'. How do you reconcile things so abhorrently offensive, oppressive and undeniably wrong?

There is a wide spectrum of what trauma is and it's a conversation my surviving sister and I have had over the years. As we were bookends standing on opposite sides of that shared past— her as the oldest and I the youngest—our stories are similar yet vastly different. The truth is, no one can share the same experience.

We must consider the age differences, the different financial contexts and the emotional states of our parents. Being just over seven years older and adhering to the rule of being kicked out by sixteen meant that I was nine years old when she left. I was twelve when Keily left and fourteen when Chris left; I was an only child for many years at home.

From Heidi's point of view, she had it worse, having to set an example and getting the brunt of the physical abuse. She regularly got king hit on the back of her head by Father's hard fist at full force. He'd sneak up on her while she was watching TV, just walking down the hallway or reading a book. The incidents were without provocation, just a reminder of how she was a failure and how useless and stupid she was for not setting the right example. Chris got verbal annihilation, constant attacks and reminders that in spite of his exceptional achievements, he was and could never be enough. Keily was likely sexually abused, as all suspected that for years he aggressively abused her for spending his money and it was part of some payoff for keeping his secrets. I wasn't physically or sexually abused, but I got guns, threats to my life and witnessed threats to my mother's life. I had the progression of alcoholism and the role of saving Mother. I was there for years, mostly alone, during the time they were progressively and chronically getting worse. In fact, I never knew my parents when they were well.

My point is, your story, my siblings' stories, my story, is enough. You don't have to defend it or make it more or less, you just need to know it's enough. There is no competition in trauma and no hierarchy, it is always insidiously damaging, but there is a way out and up.

The Act of Unforgiving

I have sat with so many others over the years as a therapist witnessing the stories they have endured. In my almost twenty five years of working in trauma and through my own experiences, I formulated a methodology that begins with a new choice, an alternate pathway one could take instead—the path to NOT forgive. Forgiving has always been the only linear path made available. Many have even said that one couldn't heal without it. That theory was formed with good intentions, but with a heavy dose of Christianity that did not consider the rights and the power most victims are striving to reclaim.

Many have been forced into sending letters, making phone calls or standing up in court and facing the person who violated them, declaring out loud they were forgiven. While for some that act may have been a powerful healer, for others, many of whom I have seen as clients, it becomes a re-injury to the wound they were so desperately trying to heal. It didn't work and they just sink deeper into their shame and into the grief that over the years slowly corrodes any hope of recovery. So, they just exist. Forgiving just couldn't absolve their pain. To heal, one must be allowed to choose. Not all perpetrators deserve to be forgiven. No second or third chances for acts so vial, consistent and destructive.

Stepping out of the contemplative mind, moving away from just a linear approach, one needs to engage the mind and the body. It is the same formula that encodes you with the pain that will encode you toward your healing. Therefore, unforgiving is a ritual involving a written declaration, symbolism and specific words to cue you in those parts that need to be heard and reintegrated, engaging all the senses through the visual, somatic and re-experiencing, and acting out where one can be heard, seen and believed.

This embodied re-enactment of standing up, declaring what is lost, what was stolen, what was violated and what was perpetrated while being witnessed by another or in the mirror by yourself is the action forward. Choose to UNFORGIVE as you reclaim and restate your right to offload those burdens, cast them out, rebuke them and send them back to their owner. Forcing the perpetrator to carry, sit with and hold their own burdens and poison. This is how one can reconcile the past and their trauma and reclaim the power that is the energy that sustains the very core of who we are. This is what trauma needs. Unforgiving keeps the victims above the line that divides hope from hopelessness, voice from rage, contentment from fear and empowerment from embitterment.

Change is hard for anyone, but especially for a child of abuse. There is an opposing contradictory thought that a child of abuse seeks consistency and change unconsciously, whether it's sabotage, entrapment or enlightenment. It sets us up for perpetual seeking: seeking love, seeking a home, seeking acceptance, seeking reassurance, seeking happiness, seeking stability, seeking who we are, seeking quiet and seeking without knowing what we are seeking.

The hardest thing for a child of trauma is living in the mundane; it feels boring, scary and uncertain. A lifetime of constant hyperarousal is the only normal known. Once confronted by what true normal looks like, it can be very destabilising as it feels uncomfortable, unfamiliar or unsafe. It is those emotions that make one lean toward what they know, perpetuating the cycle of abuse. One, therefore, must learn to sit in the uncomfortable until it becomes more malleable. It takes longer to adjust. Running, freezing, numbing, hiding or fighting our emotions left for so long then finally finding ourselves feels unnerving, disorientating and frightening. The fear is all those emotions threatening to bury us alive. Therefore walking, meditating, singing, swimming, dancing, lifting weights, writing, creating, hypnosis, psychodrama and any other tactile, embodied approach are imperative as it lessens the load, allowing one to wade through the debris slowly, succinctly, with grace and at their own pace. The mind needs this slower pace.

I have used movement my entire life to release, express, inspire and connect to those parts of me that needed to be heard. I have gone running through many countries, beaches and forests since I was eighteen years old. I remember a partner who always asked, 'Deirdre, what are you running away from?' I always answered, 'I'm running *to*; I'm running to myself.'

Through the years of my passionate pursuits of self-awareness, self-healing and the healing pathways for others, I devoured philosophy, psychoanalyst, self-actualisation and psychodrama and was always striving to become more. Do more, heal more, understand more, inspire more, create more and be more. It was integrated into my identity and became my life. However, in these later stages, as I'm now nearing sixty years of age, I stumbled upon a familiar name from my studies years ago, Ram Dass and his documentary *Becoming Nobody*. I was immediately pulled toward the title as for years I had deep and meaningful chats with a close friend, Dr Subarayadu Balla Kalla, an Indian acharya and scholar in philosophy, on who we are and who we aren't. He would often drop these powerful, simple messages that challenged my long-winded answers with, 'I am no one and I am everything. I am nowhere, yet I am everywhere.' I'd walk away trying to integrate that by watering my ego down to just enough presence, it kept me from getting hit by a bus. Therefore, *Becoming Nobody* felt right for my life now; another serendipitous gift sent my way.

I've been revisiting the concept of un-doing with so many words I find meaning in now and have integrated it into my work. Un-forgiving, Un-learning, un-binding, un-allowing, un-burdening and un-becoming. I would often spend time in my forest or along the boardwalk down the pier, toward the ocean, in the two places I now live, unbecoming all those things that no longer served me. Unbecoming any pressures, expectations, stress, worries, fears, assumptions and ego and instead being, embodying a new kind of peace, acceptance, self-love, calm and contentment. I am unbecoming, stripped back and feel more 'enough' than I've ever felt, more loved than I've ever needed and happier in a new form of calm I used to find uncomfortable because it never seemed to fit. The irony is it still doesn't, but it doesn't need to; it never did.

It is amazing feeling so alive in oneself you can place the armour down, knowing it isn't others you need to trust but rather yourself. Accepting there is nothing for you toward enlightenment in the external as your path to your greatest self is intrinsic. It is recognising you have the power to handle whatever comes your way and smiling as you discover most of those things aren't yours to battle. It is knowing that the pursuit of happiness isn't a thing that fits anywhere; it's just a state, a passing, fluid, embodied experiencing that comes and goes. It's rhythm, waves, energy, feeling, music and flow—and I still love to dance.

If I can leave you with one final but important message, it is this: please seek help. Reach out for therapy with someone who has the tools to help you navigate those tendrils of dark energies that lay in the undercurrents of our unresolved wounds. Unheard and unseen, they fester, feeding off the light you have left. Hiding in projections, triggers, rage and unresolved pain, they threaten to sever the ties to those you once held close. Changing shape, they seep out, destroying lives—yours and those who try to love you.

I understand that deep yearning that calls you to own your voice, stand up in your truth and express those words out of your body from where they have been held hostage. You do have the right to reclaim your power, your worth, your ability to feel and to grab hold of who you are and your place in this world. I do not, however, prescribe to the act of vomiting it onto the person you deem worthy of swallowing it. That sense of entitlement is fleeting and only connects you to a symbiotic relationship with the same dark energies you long to be rid of.

Equally, it further suggests you still require that person to absolve you and release you from their hooks to be free. No one can do that for you. You are your own rescuer and therefore your truth must be claimed ceremoniously, held up to the light and honoured in beauty and grace. It is the initiation that integrates those parts of you that are dark, different, wounded and equally beautiful, purpose-filled and enlightened. It is with this integrity you uphold a higher standard not only for yourself but for all of us who also endured unimaginable chronic abuse that so precariously kept us close to the edge.

We deserve to live in a world where people can feel safe, feel vulnerable, be honest and own who they authentically are. In fact,

I believe we are living in a world that now craves that kind of love, connection, realness and freedom.

If every person held themselves fully accountable for their own healing and rescue and consciously chose to sign a contract with themselves to ensure generational abuse got left in the past, then no one would be left to clean up someone else's mess. Imagine what your life might have been like if only you didn't have to spend so many years tidying up other's people stuff.

Being accountable begins by giving yourself permission to dig deep, step away from the outside world and go inside, into the intrinsic layers, the light and dark aspects of your truest self. Journey down bravely, knowing you can't fail at being you.

I created a model called the TR6 Model to highlight those dangerous shadow emotions we must be aware of before they take us too deep. These are what I found were the keys to why some people thrive and others die. They are the trap doors that one can fall into if they don't learn ways to re-enact, ground, flood, refocus, unforgive, unbecome, reclaim, rebuke, cast out, stand up, re-narrate, re-negotiate, re-encode the life, the person, the identity, the story of the beautiful, powerful human they were meant to be before someone or something got in the way of their original blueprint. They are:

- Reconciliation (lack of)
- Re-injury (the second wave)
- Ruminations (the never-ending, obsessive thoughts of asking why?)
- Resentment (bitter)
- Rage (the untamed fury within)
- Revenge (thoughts of wishing or planning to retaliate and get even)

The risk to one's being is getting stuck in any of these areas as it can lead to poor mental health, an increase in personality disorders, interpersonal relationship issues, attachment styles, reduced satisfaction with life, higher levels of emotional distress, physical health issues that maintain PTSD and CPTSD and being stuck in the past as a victim. A body rife with the bitter poison chewed, swallowed and ingested is death to the soul.

If a trauma victim is not able to unhook themselves from the perpetrator because there was no remorse or accountability, they risk sinking further down the ladder of lower vibrating emotions. The excessive ruminations of cycling negative thoughts can create resentments, which become embodied in the victim, further impacting their thoughts and emotions. As they sink even further down into rage, it then often turns into addictions or mental health, impacting interpersonal relationships. Lastly, revenge is the darkest place one can sit, as it can turn the victim into a sceptical, dark, embittered soul. Stay down there too long and I believe that is where disease can turn malignant. The key is to avoid going down that slippery slope of entrapment and or having the tools to pull yourself out. Anyone willing to challenge their story has the power to overcome it. As Brené Brown says, based on a quote from Theodore Roosevelt and her work on shame, empathy and vulnerability, 'You must be willing to step in the arena.'

The first question I ask my client when they come to see me is: What is your story? They always look at me, taken aback and say, 'I don't know where to begin.' To which I answer, 'That is exactly why I want you to consider it. Tell me your story from wherever you innately feel it right now. What's important, what's holding you back and what is it telling you about yourself? That's the place we can start from.'

Your identity is often buried beneath your words as the true self wades under the presenting symptoms, desperately seeking a lifeline. I use word associations, parts therapy, energy, symbolism, metaphors and rituals like invisible cords that drop down from the skies to grab hold of. Psychological anchors flood your mind and body until those old encoded ruminations drown and are replaced and empowered with tangible props, until you can see and feel new images, textures, tones, feelings and smells forming, recalibrating your senses with the reminder of who you really are. Only when this congruence between your true self and the persona is aligned can you finally be and feel authentically free.

Your story matters. Your story deserves to be heard and once out in the light, there are beautiful, powerful, deep ways we can rewrite, re-enact and re-empower you back to who you were born to be, the authentic, real self. In taking full hold of that pen yourself, you reclaim your power to rewrite the version of you who lives freely, wildly, passionately, purposefully with love, grace, honour and trust, victoriously. Write an amazing story where you are the hero, where love fills the marrow of your bones, where forever after lives in beautiful moments, where you regret nothing, transcend everything, live wildly, unforgive, feel powerful and express your most vulnerable, raw, most real, imperfectly, perfect you.

Take my hand, come stand beside me and feel these words as I shout them into your body and mind until they reach those parts of you that are ready to grab that lifeline. Get ready, stand up, shoulders back, stomach tight, legs strong, feet planted firmly on the ground, head slightly tilted back, eyes forward, now focus and lock it in. Breathe in deeply and slowly through your nose, fresh air, love, confidence, power, joy, strength, grace, grit and feel as you exhale the pain, darkness, burdens, the past, obstacles, shame, fear and worry, feeling them leaving your body.

Are you ready boots?

Start walkin!

This is Deirdrums, if you see her, say hi. She loves animals, nature, kindness and homemade cookies but most of all she loves to dance.

A happy day on our first Grand Bank boat. A picture is worth a thousand words: Father seated further away; Mother close to her children; Heidi and Keily with their eyes cast down; Chris and I still hopeful things wouldn't get worse.

Acknowledgements

A special thankyou to my partner Colin for his tireless love and support in all things I dream of. Your endless back massages, ridiculous wit, our spontaneous karaoke nights while sipping far too much shiraz and your noble country values keep me safe. You're my Viking, my half goat hybrid that so compliments our life in the forest.

To my children, I admire you so, I'm proud of you and will always be grateful for the endless love and support you give. You are my most cherished gifts, my blessing, the hope that held me in the worst of times and gave me the motivation and courage to be more, for you. I love you beyond words.

To my grandchildren, you are the light of our family, carving new beginnings, new memories. Always remember, I love you, you are enough, your story is your own to write and my wish for you is that you write the best one you could ever imagine.

To my remaining family, I love you. I'm so proud of the battles you've fought and wish an abundance of love, healing and an extraordinary life for you.

To my clients, thank you for bravely entrusting me with your stories. I admire you, I see you, I believe in you and your right to be loved, heard, seen and to live a life of purpose. Know that whilst I was working on inspiring you with the tools I hoped would heal your life, I was feeling the healing and exchange of that blessing from you. As the teacher becomes the student and the student becomes the teacher.

To any future clients, I invite you to reach out as my work is not done. I am simply changing form, looking forward to new ways of working, reaching out, sharing and exchanging the tools I hope will be the pathway toward you feeling and being you.

Symbols, Metaphor & Rituals

Symbols, Metaphor & Rituals are flashcards depicting a symbol with metaphorical meaning that gives access to psychological tools for deep change. Rituals are recommended for psychodrama exercises to enhance somatic re-experiencing in which one can re-claim their power. These flashcards embody over twenty five years of my work specialising in trauma and incorporate several modalities that fast-track complexed psychological ideas into a therapeutic system that treats the whole self. The cards are perfect for anyone pursuing self-actualisation and personal development with an emphasis on addressing survivors of trauma in a unique and powerful way. These decks will be available for purchase to the general public and I will conduct workshops for personal development. I will also provide training for therapists and counsellors on how to use the flashcards therapeutically for clients of trauma.

Coming Soon! Visit www.youareassickasyoursecrets.com or www.counselloroncall.com.au for updates on availabilty.

About the Author

Deirdre Rolfe lives in the charming lakeside country town of Daylesford, Victoria, Australia, surrounded by forest she loves. She enjoys mindful walks, swimming, gardening, creating hybrid statues, dinner parties with friends, pretending to be a wine connoisseur with Col, dancing, running, music, nature, family gatherings, playing with her three dogs (Obie, Tilly and Clarry) and talking too much. She also enjoys her daily practices of Un-becoming.

Deirdre continues to practise Psychotherapy, Counselling and Hypnotherapy online and at her private practice. She is available for public speaking, groups, training workshops and offers empowered shared table events discussing concepts from her book.

www.counselloroncall.com.au
www.youareassickasyoursecrets.com

'*A deep well of love in a desert of abuse and trauma. As a psychotherapist, Deirdre has discovered many ways to recover and to live a life worth living.*'

Phil Milligan, Psychologist

'You are as Sick as your Secrets' *is a disturbing read detailing Deirdre Rolfe's personal experiences growing up in a family experiencing multifaceted trauma, yet it is ultimately triumphant. She is a small, sensitive child in tune with nature and her surroundings, the woods and starry nights, who is relentlessly exposed to abuse hidden behind a veneer of the perfect family and middleclass affluence, the original beautifully dressed "insta" family. Deirdre confirms that abuse can occur on a luxury yacht in The Bahamas, to the click of ice in a cocktail glass, as much as in any less affluent location.*

This is, however, more than a memoir; it is a deeply personal account, "her truth" revealing family secrets which morphed with the, "verbal annihilation", "sprayed like a machine gun", the psychological, physical, sexual, and verbal attacks. The abuse in the family is multigenerational, the trauma influencing the health of the family members and their life courses. However, this sensitive, lively little girl grows into an astute, caring woman who uses many different techniques in her psychology and counselling practice to help others. The book encourages us to triumph over trauma and abuse, stand up, experience love and live a full life.'

Alison Tarrant Ellett, Author, Teacher

'Deirdre Rolfe has demonstrated in her book the importance of being open to oneself and to others on the journey of life.

She shares her life experiences in a way that is helpful for therapists, counsellors and educators to understand and to use in their own counselling practice. Deirdre delves deep into her own life journey and then is able to clearly express what needs to be done to be free from the secrets of life.

This book will be of great use to all who are endeavouring to to be of help to those in need. Deirdre provides the reader with a clarity of the pain from her early childhood and how she was able to overcome the trauma and become a counsellor to thousands in need. I highly recommend this book for students of counselling, psychology, psychiatry and therapy.'

Marilyn Rossner, PhD, EdD

My mother and I. An unbreakable bond.

9 780645 732504